THE
36 STRATAGEMS
to
LAUNCH AND
MARKET
YOUR PRODUCT

THE
36 STRATAGEMS
to
LAUNCH AND MARKET YOUR PRODUCT

Decode Ancient Chinese Wisdom for Niche Discovery, Positioning, and Unconventional Promotion

JIMMY LAI

Published by Lai House
ISBN: 978-1-968837-05-1

This is a work of nonfiction. While the events and strategies are based on
historical sources and personal experiences, the interpretation and
applications presented are the author's own.

Printed in the United States of America
First Edition
10 9 8 7 6 5 4 3 2 1

Disclaimer
This book is intended for educational and informational purposes only. The
strategies, interpretations, and examples presented reflect the author's
personal experiences and perspectives, and do not constitute professional
advice. Readers are encouraged to use their own judgment and discretion
when applying any ideas in real-world situations. The author and publisher
disclaim any liability for outcomes resulting from the use or misuse of the
content in this book.

Introduction

Hey, I'm really glad you're here.

This is the third book in my Thirty-Six Stratagems series— and for now, it's also the last one.

These three books were actually written together, because while the contexts are different, the core ideas of the Thirty-Six Stratagems are the same: timeless strategies that can be applied flexibly across all sorts of situations.

In fact, these books reflect the areas where I've personally used the Thirty-Six Stratagems the most: at work, in tricky conversations, and now, in launching and marketing products.

You can read this book on its own; you don't need to have read the others.

But if you have, you'll recognize familiar themes running through all three:

Strategy, timing, adaptability—and yes, sometimes a bit of playfulness.

Before we get into tactics, let me share a story from ancient China that perfectly captures the spirit of this book—and shows that the art of marketing is much older than we tend to think.

More than 2,000 years ago, during the Warring States period, a man named Lü Buwei—a wealthy merchant turned politician—compiled a massive book of philosophy, history, and politics called *Lüshi Chunqiu*.

When the book was complete, Lü Buwei didn't just print copies and quietly distribute them.

Instead, he made a bold move: he hung the manuscript on the towering city gate in the Qin capital and issued a public challenge.

His proclamation was extraordinary:

"Anyone who can improve this book by even a single word will receive a reward of a thousand gold pieces."

Now, this wasn't just an open invitation for feedback.

It was a masterstroke of strategic marketing.

Lü Buwei's offer sounded humble, almost self-effacing—but the real goal wasn't to gather edits.

It was to declare to the world that this work was so complete, so refined, that no one could possibly improve it.

The reward sounded generous, but it also set a subtle trap:

Anyone who tried and failed would only confirm the book's perfection.

And it worked brilliantly.

People flocked to the city gate, driven by curiosity, admiration, and yes, the allure of gold.

Scholars debated its contents, common people read it aloud in public squares, and before long, *Lüshi Chunqiu* had become a household name.

Lü Buwei didn't just publish a book—he created a cultural moment, a viral sensation in a world without printing presses, newspapers, or social media.

When I first learned this story, I couldn't help but think about how perfectly it illustrates several of the *Thirty-Six Stratagems:*

Stratagem 17: Throw a brick to attract jade (offering something small to gain something bigger)

Stratagem 10: Hide a knife behind a smile (appearing humble while asserting dominance)

Stratagem 27: Feign ignorance without going mad (pretending openness while remaining fully in control)

It's a beautiful example of how the *Thirty-Six Stratagems* weren't just battlefield tactics—they were timeless tools for influence, persuasion, and yes, marketing.

And that brings me to why I wrote this book.

In my ten years as a product director at startups, I've learned that strategy is everything—especially when resources are tight.

When you don't have massive budgets or an army of marketers, you have to rely on creativity, timing, and strategic thinking to stand out.

That means thinking about marketing from the very beginning—not just after a product is built.

Where is your niche?

Who exactly are you talking to?

How do you carve out space when you're competing with bigger players?

That's where this book begins.

The Thirty-Six Stratagems in Modern Product Launch and Marketing

There are already plenty of excellent marketing books out there.

You can find countless guides that teach frameworks like segmentation, targeting, positioning (STP), or the classic 4Ps—Product, Price, Place, Promotion.

And there's no shortage of how-to guides on digital funnels, social media strategy, content marketing, SEO best practices… you name it.

If you're looking for a step-by-step tactical manual on those topics, this isn't it.

This book is something else.

It's designed to help you when you're surrounded by all those "best practices" and you need a way to think differently—to break out of the mold and create an approach that truly fits your unique situation.

Because here's the thing:

Most people know the basics of marketing.

The real challenge isn't knowing what to do—it's figuring out how to do it in a way that feels different, that captures attention, that resonates in a crowded marketplace.

That's where the Thirty-Six Stratagems come in.

These ancient tactics aren't checklists; they're mental tools.

They help you see patterns, anticipate reactions, and uncover opportunities that others miss.

They give you hints for thinking laterally when everyone else is marching straight ahead.

This is why I find them so useful when thinking about niche markets.

In niche marketing, your biggest asset is not scale—it's precision, creativity, and timing.

You can't outspend the big players, but you can out-think them.

Let me also say this:

While I believe the Thirty-Six Stratagems are brilliant and timeless, I know that a book about them is probably not a perfect niche for the English-language market.

But I wrote this book—and this series—not because I thought it was trendy, but because I genuinely wanted to introduce this treasure of ancient Chinese wisdom to my friends and readers outside of East Asian cultural sphere.

After this book is published, I will, at some point, of course, use some of the very strategies inside to market it.

But if, in the end, it doesn't sell particularly well... well, maybe that just proves this topic itself isn't a perfect niche after all.

The market is always an unknown challenge—and no one knows what will happen until they try.

For me, though, even if just a small number of English-speaking readers enjoy these books, it will have been worth it.

I have no regrets about spending the time to create this series and share this unique part of Chinese heritage with the English-speaking world.

Let's get started.

Table of Contents

勝戰計

PART 1: Winning Stratagems

Strategies used when you have the upper hand

瞞天過海

1. Deceive the Heavens to Cross the Sea

Core Idea

This classic stratagem is all about hiding a bold move in plain sight. The name comes from an old story about tricking someone while appearing completely ordinary—crossing the sea under the open sky, as if there's nothing unusual going on. The idea is to take advantage of people's tendency to overlook what feels familiar. When something appears routine or mundane, it rarely raises alarms—even when something important is happening beneath the surface.

In psychological terms, this is about cognitive bias. People focus on what's new or unusual and often ignore what they assume they already understand. By wrapping your true intentions in something predictable or traditional, you reduce suspicion and make progress without triggering resistance.

This stratagem is not about deception for harm; it's about strategic presentation. Sometimes, the best way to get something important done is to make it look... ordinary.

Historical Example

One of the most famous stories behind this stratagem comes from the Tang Dynasty. General Xue Rengui, serving under Emperor Taizong, was preparing for a naval invasion against the kingdom of Goguryeo. To prevent the enemy from noticing, he ordered his troops to conduct repeated drills—boarding and disembarking from ships every day in full view of the enemy.

After several days, the routine seemed so ordinary that no one paid it any attention. Then one morning, under the same routine, the army set sail for real—crossing the sea without alerting the enemy.

Modern Marketing Scenario

Not every product needs a drumroll. Sometimes, the smartest move is to launch under the radar—making it feel like just another post, feature, or update, while it quietly does something bigger.

A solo developer builds a free Notion template and shares it on Reddit. Inside is a subtle link to her paid app—no big pitch, just curiosity-driven clicks. A café tests a seasonal drink by calling it "Barista's Pick," not "New Item." The name makes it feel like part of the regular flow, so no one resists trying it.

The point isn't to hide what you're doing—it's to wrap it in something familiar, low-pressure, and unthreatening. That way, by the time people notice what's really happening, they already like it.

In marketing, invisibility can buy you time, traction, and trust—without setting off alarms.

Practice Scenarios: Apply the Stratagem

Scenario 1: The Unassuming Soft Launch

You're releasing a niche productivity tool, but you worry that announcing it too loudly will attract copycats before you gain traction.

Your Challenge: How could you launch through a free template, demo video, or related micro-product that feels casual—while subtly introducing your real offering?

Scenario 2: The Educator with a Secret Agenda

You're a piano teacher who just created a digital course for beginners, but your audience only follows you for free YouTube tutorials.

Your Challenge: How might you build your course promotion into a normal tutorial video—positioning it as "just a deeper dive" for those who are interested, without triggering resistance?

Scenario 3: The Market Research in Disguise

You want to validate a skincare product idea, but launching a full brand feels risky and expensive.

Your Challenge: What simple blog, giveaway, or online poll could you create that looks like generic content—but secretly helps you test market demand, pricing, and audience language?

圍魏救趙

2. Relieve the Besieged by Attacking the Base

Core Idea

This stratagem suggests solving a problem indirectly by targeting something your opponent values more. Rather than confronting the enemy head-on, you force them to back off by threatening something else they can't afford to lose.

At its heart, this strategy is about shifting pressure.

If someone is blocking your way, find what they're protecting, what they're vulnerable to, or what they can't ignore—and move your effort there.

This way, you turn their strength into a weakness.

Historical Example

The origin of this tactic comes from the Warring States period in ancient China. When the State of Zhao was under siege by the State of Wei, the allied State of Qi didn't send troops directly to help Zhao.

Instead, General Sun Bin led his forces to attack Wei's capital.

Wei had no choice but to lift the siege and rush back to protect its own territory. By threatening something more vital, Qi achieved its goal without direct confrontation.

Modern Marketing Scenario

Sometimes, trying to win over your target customer directly just doesn't work. They're resistant, distracted, or already loyal to another brand. So instead of banging on the front door, you shift your attention to something—or someone—they care even more about.

Say you're launching a kids' toothbrush, but parents aren't biting. They've seen too many gimmicks. So you stop trying to sell the brush itself and instead run a content campaign on kids' bedtime routines. You partner with sleep experts, pediatricians, and parenting bloggers. The toothbrush just happens to be part of the toolkit. By reframing the conversation around sleep, you earn parents' trust—and get them to lower their defenses. Or you're building an AI writing tool, but writers are skeptical. So you pivot your outreach to writing coaches and educators who influence them. Convince the influencers, and the writers follow.

This stratagem is about indirect pressure. When someone resists your message, don't fight them head-on. Shift the battlefield. Go after what they care about most—and watch them move.

Practice Scenarios: Apply the Stratagem

Scenario 1: The Resistant Buyer

You're selling a new meal planning app, but busy moms aren't downloading it.

Your Challenge: What related problem—like grocery budgeting or picky eating—could you focus on first to gain attention and build trust?

Scenario 2: The Skeptical Community

You've made a tool for independent authors, but they're wary of automation.

Your Challenge: How might you win over editors, writing coaches, or author YouTubers who those authors already trust?

Scenario 3: The Competitive Category

You're launching a supplement in a crowded wellness market, but you can't outspend the major brands.

Your Challenge: Where could you shift the narrative—maybe to gut health, mental clarity, or daily energy—to connect more deeply with what customers actually prioritize?

借刀殺人

3. Kill with a Borrowed Knife

Core Idea

This stratagem suggests using someone else's power, influence, or resources to accomplish your own goals—especially when it comes to confronting difficult problems or people.

Rather than taking risks yourself, you find a way to let others act on your behalf.

It teaches us that you don't always need to confront an issue directly—sometimes it's more efficient (and less risky) to achieve your goals by leveraging others' authority, energy, or ambitions.

Historical Example

The phrase "Kill with a borrowed knife" comes from the idea that the most effective attack is one carried out by someone else, while you remain safe and uninvolved.

In ancient China, political rivals would often pit one enemy against another to weaken both sides.

A notable example involves the cunning strategist Fan Li, who manipulated rival states into weakening each other, saving his own state from direct conflict.

Modern Marketing Scenario

Why fight resistance when someone else can do it for you? This stratagem is about borrowing credibility, reach, or authority to do what you can't (yet) do on your own. Not every message needs to come from you—sometimes, the most persuasive voice is someone else's.

Let's say you've created a sustainable cleaning product, but consumers don't trust new eco claims anymore. Instead of pitching it yourself, you get a respected cleaning influencer to share it as part of their morning routine. Suddenly, it's not you telling people it works—it's someone they already follow. Or maybe you've built a budgeting tool for college students, but they don't want another app. So you team up with a popular personal finance TikToker. The influencer does the talking; you do the converting.

You can also "borrow the knife" through platforms—launching your online course through a trusted marketplace like Skillshare instead of trying to build your own credibility from scratch. This isn't about hiding. It's about recognizing when someone else is better positioned to open the door you want to walk through.

Practice Scenarios: Apply the Stratagem

Scenario 1: The Untrusted Voice

You're promoting a healthy snack brand, but people think it's just another processed food.

Your Challenge: Who could you partner with—a fitness coach, dietitian, or school program—who has the trust you haven't yet earned?

Scenario 2: The Saturated Feed

You run a small lifestyle brand, but social ads aren't working anymore.

Your Challenge: What voices or communities could you tap into—like micro-influencers or curated newsletters—so the pitch doesn't have to come from you?

Scenario 3: The Conversion Block

You've built a great app, but your landing page traffic just isn't converting.

Your Challenge: Could you integrate your product into someone else's workflow, marketplace, or onboarding funnel, so users encounter it where trust already exists?

以逸待勞

4. Wait at ease for the weary enemy

Core Idea

This stratagem is about conserving your energy while your opponent exhausts theirs.

You don't need to react to every challenge immediately. Sometimes, the wisest move is to wait—calmly, deliberately—while others rush in and burn out.

At its core, this strategy teaches the value of restraint, preparation, and timing.

In today's fast-paced world, the person who stays grounded often has the clearest view of the battlefield.

Historical Example

The phrase originates from Sun Tzu's idea of choosing the time and place of battle.

A classic example is the Battle of Red Cliffs. Rather than confront the much larger enemy head-on, the allied forces waited until the opposing fleet was weakened by poor preparation and long supply lines. When the time was right, they launched a decisive attack—and won.

Victory didn't come from brute strength. It came from patience and timing.

Modern Marketing Scenario

Speed isn't always an advantage—especially when your competitors are wearing themselves out. In business, there's a tendency to rush: launch quickly, post constantly, iterate fast. But this stratagem reminds us that patience can be the ultimate strategy—especially when others are burning out trying to "move fast and break things."

Imagine you're in a niche where competitors are constantly pivoting—changing their features, pricing, and messaging every other month. You hold steady. You watch. You listen. You keep your product simple and clear, while they exhaust their budgets chasing trends. Then, when users start looking for stability, you're the one who feels trustworthy.

Or take the example of a slow-content brand: while competitors push daily posts on five platforms, this team publishes one thoughtful essay a month. Their audience? Smaller, but more loyal—and growing.

Waiting doesn't mean doing nothing. It means preparing calmly while others scramble. When the right moment comes, you'll be rested, clear-headed, and ready to strike.

Practice Scenarios: Apply the Stratagem

Scenario 1: The Trend-Chasing Competitors

Your competitors are rapidly changing their messaging to keep up with fads.

Your Challenge: How could you maintain a consistent brand presence—calm and focused—so that when users get overwhelmed, you're the stable alternative?

Scenario 2: The Overposting Race

You're a solo creator feeling pressure to post every day just to stay relevant.

Your Challenge: What's one slower, deeper form of content—like a weekly newsletter or monthly deep-dive—that could set you apart instead of draining your energy?

Scenario 3: The Market in Flux

You've been eyeing a new niche, but it's currently flooded with hype-driven launches.

Your Challenge: How can you quietly build foundational assets now—like SEO content, referral partnerships, or audience research—so you're ready when the dust settles?

趁火打劫

5. Loot a Burning House

Core Idea

This stratagem advises you to seize opportunities when your opponent is in chaos or weakened.

The metaphor is clear: if a house is on fire, the people inside are distracted—now is the time to take what you want. In other words, strike when your rivals are vulnerable and can't defend themselves effectively.

This strategy may seem harsh, but it reminds us that timing is everything. Life—and especially competition—is not always fair.

If you wait for perfect conditions, you may miss your window. But if you act when others are distracted, you may win with less resistance.

Historical Example

This tactic appears in countless battles. A well-known example comes from the Warring States period in ancient China.

When the State of Qi fell into political turmoil after the death of its ruler, the neighboring State of Yan launched an unexpected attack. Qi, distracted and disorganized, couldn't defend itself—and suffered a devastating loss.

The lesson: when an enemy is preoccupied with internal issues, external threats strike harder and with greater effect.

Modern Marketing Scenario

When the market is on fire, most people panic or freeze. But for you, chaos might be the perfect moment to act.

This stratagem is about striking while others are distracted—launching, pivoting, or expanding at a moment when competitors are too busy managing their own crises to notice.

Let's say a bigger brand in your space just went through a messy PR disaster. Everyone's watching them stumble. You quietly roll out a competing product with friendlier branding, smoother onboarding, and a warm, personal launch message. While their fire rages, you're moving in, unnoticed.

Or maybe the economy just shifted, and your competitors are slashing budgets. Instead of retreating, you double down on community building—offering free tools, webinars, or support while others go silent. You don't need to be loud. You just need to be there.

Timing is everything. And in marketing, "bad times" are often wide-open doors—if you're brave enough to walk through them.

Practice Scenarios: Apply the Stratagem

Scenario 1: The Downfall of a Giant

A leading competitor is getting backlash for a tone-deaf ad campaign.

Your Challenge: How could you quietly highlight your values or launch a campaign that contrasts theirs—without explicitly calling them out?

Scenario 2: The Funding Freeze

During an economic downturn, most startups are freezing content budgets.

Your Challenge: What low-cost, high-impact content or outreach could you deploy right now while attention is cheap and competition is distracted?

Scenario 3: The Audience Exodus

A big platform or brand is making unpopular changes, and their users are looking for alternatives.

Your Challenge: How might you create a landing page, tweet thread, or offer that speaks directly to those frustrated users—inviting them in while others stay quiet?

聲東擊西

6. Make a Feint to the East While Attacking in the West

Core Idea

This stratagem teaches the value of deception and misdirection: draw attention to one place, then strike somewhere else.

The key principle is to confuse your opponent or audience, so they focus their resources in the wrong direction—leaving your true goal unguarded.

At its heart, this stratagem is about controlling perception. Success doesn't always require brute force—sometimes, it just takes knowing where people are looking, and deliberately shifting their gaze.

Historical Example

The strategy comes from ancient Chinese warfare, where misleading troop movements were a common tactic. A well-known example comes from the Three Kingdoms period, when strategist Zhou Yu tricked Cao Cao by creating the illusion of a frontal naval attack, while secretly sending his real forces through an alternate path. The decoy drew Cao Cao's attention, and the real strike landed where he was unprepared.

This tactic allowed Zhou Yu to win a crucial victory not by strength, but by redirection and surprise.

Modern Marketing Scenario

Distraction can be a strategy. If your audience—or your competitors—are focused on one thing, you can quietly win elsewhere.

This stratagem is all about misdirection. In marketing, that might mean pulling attention toward something fun, light, or even unrelated—so that your real move lands without resistance.

For example, you might tease a flashy product update that gets everyone talking, while your actual priority is launching a new pricing model. Or you publish a fun quiz on social media that draws traffic, but the real purpose is to drive email signups through the quiz result page.

One indie game developer posted memes for weeks while quietly building buzz for an in-game event. Everyone thought they were just goofing off—until launch day, when thousands showed up.

Misdirection isn't deception. It's timing and perception. While others look left, you move right.

Practice Scenarios: Apply the Stratagem

Scenario 1: The Flashy Decoy

You're planning a major pricing change, but your users resist anything "salesy."

Your Challenge: What smaller update—like a new feature or design refresh—could you spotlight to draw attention while rolling out the pricing change in the background?

Scenario 2: The Fun Lead Magnet

You're launching a new coaching program, but a direct sales pitch feels too pushy for your audience.

Your Challenge: Could you create a fun quiz, challenge, or resource that's more playful—while still guiding people toward your offer?

Scenario 3: The Launch Distraction

A competitor is preparing a big launch and hogging all the attention.

Your Challenge: What surprising angle—like a behind-the-scenes story or viral side project—could you release at the same time to shift the spotlight just enough to earn clicks and curiosity?

敵戰計

PART 2: Enemy Dealing Stratagems

Strategies for facing an equal or stronger enemy

無中生有

7. Create Something from Nothing

Core Idea

This stratagem centers on the power of perception. It encourages you to fabricate a narrative, opportunity, or resource—even if it doesn't yet exist—so convincingly that others begin to treat it as real. By shaping belief, you shape reality.

The phrase "Create Something from Nothing" reminds us that in both strategy and daily life, people respond more to perception than truth. If you present an illusion with confidence and consistency, others may adjust their behavior as if it were fact. Over time, that illusion can take on a life of its own.

At its heart, this stratagem is about using imagination and confidence to bend situations in your favor—especially when you have few resources or little leverage.

Historical Example

A classic story from ancient China involves strategist Zhang Yi during the Warring States period. Sent to convince the powerful State of Chu to abandon its alliance with Qi, Zhang Yi arrived with no gifts or army—just persuasive words. He fabricated the promise of territory from the rival State of Qin, a promise he had no authority or ability to fulfill. But he spoke with such detail and conviction that the king of Chu believed him and switched allegiances. Though the land never came, the alliance was broken, and Qin gained the advantage.

Zhang Yi's empty promise reshaped the political map—proof that belief alone can move mountains.

Modern Marketing Scenario

What if your product doesn't really exist yet—but people start acting like it does? This stratagem is about perception: creating buzz, demand, or authority before you've actually built the thing. In niche marketing, especially, belief can precede reality—and shape it. A solo maker announces an "invite-only" writing app that doesn't exist yet. The landing page is polished, the waitlist is real, and early signups get access to "limited alpha slots." Within days, hundreds join. Now, there's proof of demand—before a line of code is written.

In fashion, creators release mood boards and mockups before manufacturing begins. The comments, shares, and DMs help them decide which pieces are worth producing. The designs feel real—because the audience wants them to be.

And in the online course space, creators often pre-sell a program with just a title, a promise, and a few testimonials from beta testers. People buy into the vision, not just the content. Done right, this isn't about faking it. It's about believing so clearly in your value that others start believing too—and moving as if it's already here.

Practice Scenarios: Apply the Stratagem

Scenario 1: The Landing Page Test

You have an idea for a productivity app but haven't built anything yet.

Your Challenge: How might you create a simple, elegant waitlist page that presents the app as real—so you can gauge genuine interest before investing time?

Scenario 2: The Pre-Sale Play

You want to launch a paid newsletter but aren't sure if there's demand.

Your Challenge: Could you write a sample issue, share a vision statement, and offer founding memberships—so early adopters shape the product with you?

Scenario 3: The Imagined Brand

You're exploring a niche skincare line but can't afford manufacturing upfront.

Your Challenge: What if you launched the brand visually first—mockups, vibe videos, packaging previews—and used engagement to decide what to actually produce?

暗渡陳倉

8. Sneak Through the Back Route

Core Idea

This stratagem is about tactical redirection. When direct confrontation would be costly—or simply impossible—it urges you to seek an alternate route that avoids resistance altogether.

Rather than masking your intention (as in Stratagem 1), this one focuses on avoiding the strongest point of opposition. It asks: Why attack the front when the side or rear is unguarded? In any system—military, political, or corporate—there are always weak spots, overlooked gates, or less-defended paths. This stratagem teaches you to find and use them.

It's not a trick—it's leverage. It's about understanding how to shift your path, not your purpose, and still reach the same goal.

Historical Example

During the Tang dynasty, the famous general Li Shiji was once tasked with defeating a well-defended rebel fortress. A direct assault would have cost thousands of lives. Instead of launching a frontal attack, Li sent scouts to find an unguarded path through the mountains behind the fortress.

After days of quiet maneuvering, his troops descended unexpectedly from the rear, forcing the enemy into disarray and surrender—without ever breaching the front gates.

Li's approach didn't disguise his goal; it simply found a better way to reach it.

Modern Marketing Scenario

Sometimes the front door is locked—and everyone's watching it. That's your cue to find a side entrance no one's guarding.

This stratagem is about avoiding resistance by changing your path, not your purpose. In marketing, it means reaching your customer in a way they didn't expect... but are totally open to.

A new language learning app struggles to get traction in the crowded "productivity tools" category. So instead of advertising as a study app, it's rebranded as a daily habit tracker with a language twist. Same goal, different framing—and suddenly it appeals to people browsing for habit tools, not just education.

Or a solopreneur can't get traction promoting her new paid community for writers. So she starts a weekly "Write With Me" livestream on YouTube. No pitch, no hard sell—just showing up consistently. Over time, the community asks how they can join her private space.

You're not hiding your mission. You're finding the route with the fewest guards.

Practice Scenarios: Apply the Stratagem

Scenario 1: The Framing Shift

You're offering a course on creative writing, but people think it's too academic.

Your Challenge: How could you reposition it—as a "story therapy" program, or "content strategy bootcamp"—to tap into a different desire?

Scenario 2: The Platform Detour

You're having trouble getting newsletter signups from Twitter.

Your Challenge: Could you host short AMAs or giveaways on niche forums or Discord servers, where the noise is lower and people are more receptive?

Scenario 3: The Soft Introduction

You've built a high-ticket coaching program, but cold emails aren't working.

Your Challenge: How might you design a free mini-audit, quiz, or workbook that leads people in through curiosity—without making them feel like they're being sold?

隔岸觀火

9. Watch the fire from the other shore

Core Idea

This stratagem advises patience and observation. Rather than rushing into conflict, it encourages you to stand back and let opposing forces exhaust themselves. By remaining on the sidelines, you can gather information, avoid unnecessary risk, and wait for the right moment to act.

The phrase conjures an image: two armies fighting across the river while you stand safely on your side, watching the chaos unfold. In many cases, the wisest move is to observe until others reveal their weaknesses—or destroy themselves without your involvement.

This is a strategy of restraint. It's especially powerful when you're not the strongest player, or when a situation is still too volatile to influence. By waiting, you conserve energy and maintain clarity while others burn theirs.

Historical Example

During the late Eastern Han dynasty, warlords Cao Cao and Yuan Shao prepared for battle. Liu Bei, a smaller regional leader at the time, was urged to join one side. But instead of picking a team, Liu Bei chose to retreat to a neutral position and observe. He watched as Yuan Shao, despite having superior numbers, made poor decisions and was ultimately defeated by Cao Cao. Only after the tides turned did Liu Bei begin to act—by then, he had a clearer view of the new power structure and moved forward with stronger alliances. Liu Bei's decision to "watch the fire from across the river" preserved his forces and gave him the strategic clarity needed to survive and eventually thrive.

Modern Marketing Scenario

Not every battle needs your sword. Sometimes, your best move is to stand back, observe—and let others burn themselves out.

In marketing, this means resisting the urge to jump into every trend, debate, or launch rush. Instead, you study how the chaos plays out—so you can move with clarity when the smoke clears.

Say your competitors are all racing to adopt a hot new platform—Threads, Clubhouse, whatever's trending. You hold back. You watch what kinds of content actually perform, what pitfalls others run into, what the users really care about. Then, two months later, you arrive with a focused campaign that feels deliberate—because it is.

Or imagine two influencers in your niche go to war over tactics. While their audiences split and argue, you quietly put out a thoughtful blog post that addresses both perspectives with nuance. You're not taking sides—you're gaining trust.

Sometimes, staying quiet is not passivity—it's positioning.

Practice Scenarios: Apply the Stratagem

Scenario 1: The Platform Hype Cycle

A new social platform is exploding, and everyone's jumping on.

Your Challenge: How can you monitor what actually works before investing time—so you enter with precision, not panic?

Scenario 2: The Expert Flame War

Thought leaders in your space are clashing publicly over strategy.

Your Challenge: Could you publish a calm, helpful take that summarizes the situation for confused newcomers—and win fans by staying above the noise?

Scenario 3: The Trend-Fueled Chaos

Everyone is launching AI tools with wild promises, but user trust is dropping fast.

Your Challenge: How might you position your product as the "clear, stable, trustworthy" option—after the dust settles?

笑裡藏刀

10. Hide a Knife Behind a Smile

Core Idea

This stratagem warns us of the danger—and power—of masking hostility with friendliness. On the surface, it appears to promote deception, but its deeper insight lies in understanding that people often lower their guard in the face of charm, politeness, or familiarity. When tensions are high or stakes are great, presenting a calm and friendly exterior can disarm your opponent—emotionally or strategically—until you're ready to act.

"Hide a knife behind a smile" doesn't always mean literal betrayal; sometimes it means preparing for a confrontation while avoiding unnecessary escalation. It's about keeping your true intentions concealed until the right moment—especially when you're in a weaker position.

Historical Example

During the late Han dynasty, the warlord Cao Cao famously invited political rival Dong Cheng to a banquet. With a pleasant face and gentle conversation, Cao Cao made no mention of Dong Cheng's betrayal—though he had already discovered the conspiracy. Only after the banquet, when the atmosphere of friendship had softened resistance, did Cao Cao arrest Dong Cheng and execute the traitors.

This chilling moment in Chinese history illustrates how a mask of civility can be used to delay panic and opposition until action is inevitable.

Modern Marketing Scenario

Sometimes, the most persuasive message isn't loud or aggressive—it's friendly, casual, even charming. But under that friendly tone? Strategy.

This stratagem is about pairing a soft front with a sharp move. In marketing, that often means delivering something disruptive or bold—but wrapping it in warmth, humor, or storytelling so it's easier to swallow.

A startup launches a pricing increase, but doesn't announce "We're raising rates." Instead, they send a newsletter titled: "Biggest update since coffee in the breakroom ☕"—with fun visuals, user success stories, and a warm explanation of how the new pricing supports better service. Users feel informed, not ambushed. Or a solo creator wants to shut down a free-tier offer, but knows the backlash could hurt. So they post a heartfelt blog titled "What I learned giving away my work for free for 3 years," filled with transparency, gratitude, and a subtle pivot to paid options.

This stratagem isn't about deceit—it's about emotional intelligence. You can say hard things. Just say them with a smile.

Practice Scenarios: Apply the Stratagem

Scenario 1: The Unpopular Change

You need to sunset a feature that a vocal group of users loves.

Your Challenge: How might you communicate the change in a way that feels thoughtful, transparent, and empathetic—rather than cold or corporate?

Scenario 2: The Strategic Apology

A campaign flopped and users are annoyed.

Your Challenge: What kind of light, self-aware messaging could turn frustration into forgiveness—while reinforcing your brand's voice?

Scenario 3: The Bold Shift

You're repositioning your brand toward a more premium offering, but long-time users may feel alienated.

Your Challenge: How could you wrap this shift in a story—of growth, evolution, and shared values—so it feels exciting, not exclusionary?

李代桃僵

11. Sacrifice the Plum Tree to Save the Peach

Core Idea

This stratagem teaches the value of strategic sacrifice. When faced with a difficult choice, sometimes preserving the whole requires letting go of a part. You may choose to give up a less critical asset, take a small loss, or even let someone take the blame—so that something more important can survive or thrive.

The idea isn't to be ruthless, but to understand what must be protected at all costs, and what can be traded away to ensure that. It's about prioritizing the greater good or long-term success, even at the cost of short-term damage.

In short: sometimes, to save the peach tree, you have to cut the plum.

Historical Example

During the late Eastern Han dynasty, the powerful warlord Cao Cao faced a crisis. One of his top generals, Xiahou Dun, accidentally killed a civilian while trying to enforce discipline. The incident enraged the local population, threatening to spark rebellion and undermine Cao Cao's fragile rule. Cao Cao made a bold decision—he publicly punished Xiahou Dun, his own loyal general, by demoting him and issuing an apology to the people. In truth, he didn't intend to abandon his general; he later restored his position quietly. But by "sacrificing" Xiahou Dun in public, Cao Cao preserved the greater stability of his territory. The general took a hit, but the kingdom was saved.

Modern Marketing Scenario

Sometimes, you need to let go of something small to protect something bigger. This stratagem is all about strategic sacrifice—cutting features, abandoning products, or even admitting mistakes in order to preserve your core offering, your brand trust, or your long-term growth.

Let's say you're running a SaaS platform with multiple tools, but one feature is eating up support time and barely used. You quietly phase it out, even though a small group of users complains. Why? Because it frees your team to double down on the product's true strength—and deliver more value to your core market.

Or a digital creator realizes their older content is outdated and hurting SEO. They archive dozens of blog posts, knowing that trimming weak material will boost authority and clarity. Less is more—especially when what's left is strong.

The key is knowing what matters most. You don't sacrifice randomly—you sacrifice intentionally, to protect what truly moves your business forward.

Practice Scenarios: Apply the Stratagem

Scenario 1: The Feature That Had to Go

You're maintaining an old legacy feature that a small group still uses, but it slows development.

Your Challenge: How could you sunset it in a way that preserves goodwill—while clearly communicating why the change is a long-term benefit?

Scenario 2: The Abandoned Product Line

One of your products just isn't selling, but you've invested a lot into it.

Your Challenge: What messaging or internal reframing could help you cut your losses—so you can refocus on what actually works?

Scenario 3: The Pricing Trade-off

You want to simplify your pricing model, but removing the lowest tier might upset some early users.

Your Challenge: How can you reframe this change as an upgrade in service or simplicity—while minimizing damage to user trust?

順手牽羊

12. Take the Opportunity to Pilfer a Goat

Core Idea

This stratagem is about recognizing and seizing unexpected opportunities—especially when others are distracted or unaware. The phrase "Take the opportunity to pilfer a goat" evokes a vivid image: you're passing through someone's pasture, and in the chaos or neglect, you quietly lead a goat away. It's a small gain, taken when no one's looking.

This strategy teaches us to act swiftly and decisively when an unguarded advantage presents itself. It doesn't require deception or conflict—just attentiveness and a willingness to capitalize on timing.

It also reminds us that opportunities don't always arrive with trumpets and fanfare. They often appear quietly, disguised as minor gaps, overlooked resources, or moments of distraction.

Historical Example

During the Three Kingdoms era, the brilliant tactician Zhuge Liang once led a northern campaign against the Wei kingdom. In one battle, his army encountered a supply shortage. Rather than fight for territory, he diverted a small force to exploit a weakness in a nearby enemy outpost, capturing vital supplies with minimal conflict.

It wasn't a major victory, but it bought his army time and kept morale high. By noticing a small vulnerability and acting on it, Zhuge Liang improved his position without risking a major confrontation.

Modern Marketing Scenario

Opportunities don't always announce themselves. Sometimes, they just wander by—quietly, casually—and all you have to do is reach out and take them. This stratagem is about recognizing and acting on small, low-resistance chances to gain attention, users, or trust. It's not about stealing. It's about noticing what others miss—and moving quickly.

A new fitness coach sees a Reddit thread where dozens of users complain about confusing macros. She replies with a friendly comment and links to her free "macro cheat sheet." No sales pitch, no campaign—just the right offer in the right moment. Over a hundred signups in two days. Or a solopreneur notices that a major newsletter in her niche is unexpectedly looking for guest contributors. She drops everything and submits a tailored piece that includes a subtle mention of her product. That post becomes her top traffic source for months.

"Pilfering the goat" isn't random—it's strategic responsiveness. Stay alert. When people lower their guard, help them. And if they say thank you with their attention, great. That goat's yours now.

Practice Scenarios: Apply the Stratagem

Scenario 1: The Missed Mention

A niche influencer casually mentions a problem your product solves—but doesn't name you.

Your Challenge: How could you step in gently—via comment, DM, or share—with something helpful that introduces your brand naturally?

Scenario 2: The Open Door

A podcast you admire suddenly opens up guest pitches for the first time.

Your Challenge: What story, lesson, or perspective could you offer that provides genuine value—and quietly brings in your product or brand?

Scenario 3: The Trending Topic

A viral trend hits your niche, and everyone's reacting.

Your Challenge: How might you join the conversation fast—with a free tool, meme, or offer—that connects naturally to your product while people are still paying attention?

攻戰計

PART 3: Attacking Stratagems

Strategies for direct confrontation
and power struggles

打草驚蛇

13. Stir the Grass to Scare the Snake

Core Idea

This stratagem is about probing your opponent to reveal hidden threats, intentions, or defenses. By making a subtle move—just enough to cause a reaction—you can detect danger before walking into it blindly.

"Stir the grass to scare the snake" warns against proceeding into uncertain territory without first testing the waters. It's a cautionary tactic: better to wake the snake now and see where it hides than step directly into its bite. The idea is not to attack but to observe what emerges.

This stratagem is especially useful when you're unsure of the full situation. Stir things up just enough to trigger a response. That response will tell you everything you need to know.

Historical Example

In the late Tang dynasty, General Li Keyong was suspicious of a subordinate who appeared loyal but had once rebelled.

Instead of confronting him directly, Li Keyong sent an envoy with a deliberately ambiguous message.

When the subordinate panicked and fled, his betrayal was confirmed.

Li had stirred the grass—and the snake revealed itself.

Modern Marketing Scenario

Before you launch something big, poke the market. Gently.

This stratagem is about using small actions to reveal hidden objections, unmet needs, or potential threats—before you commit. In marketing, that means testing the waters: running small experiments to see what stirs.

Let's say you're thinking about entering the pet accessories market. Instead of building a full product line, you post a few concept sketches on Instagram, then run a poll: "Which one would you buy?" The comments reveal not only preferences— but strong opinions about pricing, safety, and eco-materials. You've just spotted the snakes in the grass.

Or maybe you're unsure whether your SaaS tool's new AI feature will be well received. You quietly add a toggle marked "beta" and monitor how many users click it, how long they stay, and what support tickets roll in. The feedback tells you what the official launch never would.

A little friction now can save you a costly surprise later.

Practice Scenarios: Apply the Stratagem

Scenario 1: The Opinion Probe

You're planning a book on remote work culture but aren't sure how readers will react to your core thesis.

Your Challenge: What kind of tweet, blog post, or short video could you publish to provoke reactions—and reveal where people agree or push back?

Scenario 2: The Feature Tease

You're designing a new premium feature, but it might spark backlash.

Your Challenge: How might you pre-release a limited version (or just the settings toggle) to observe adoption and surface concerns quietly?

Scenario 3: The Niche Test

You're exploring a new customer segment but aren't sure it's viable.

Your Challenge: Could you run a targeted ad, micro-survey, or lead magnet just for that group—to gauge interest before building anything?

借屍還魂

14. Revive the Dead to Return the Soul

Core Idea

This stratagem involves bringing back an old concept, strategy, or symbol—something thought to be obsolete or forgotten—and giving it new life and purpose. It's about reusing the past in a way that serves the present, leveraging nostalgia, legacy, or forgotten assets to create unexpected impact.

By "reviving the dead," you're not just recycling; you're recontextualizing. Something dismissed as irrelevant can suddenly become powerful when applied to new circumstances. People are often caught off guard by what they assume is no longer relevant.

This strategy works well when the environment has changed but people's assumptions haven't. Surprise them by breathing new life into something they thought they understood.

Historical Example

During the early Han Dynasty, the strategist Zhang Liang helped Emperor Liu Bang consolidate power. At one point, Zhang Liang suggested reinstating certain ceremonial practices from the former Qin Dynasty—rituals that had been widely despised.

However, by subtly reviving these rituals in a modified form and presenting them as symbols of unity and continuity, Zhang Liang helped stabilize the new regime. What had once been a tool of oppression was repurposed into a sign of legitimacy and order. The "soul" of authority returned through a "dead" tradition.

Modern Marketing Scenario

Not every idea needs to be original. Sometimes, the smartest marketing move is to resurrect something that once worked—then breathe new life into it.

This stratagem is perfect for founders, creators, and marketers looking for momentum. You spot a product that flopped because it was ahead of its time. Or a forgotten blog post that suddenly feels relevant again. Or an old-school sales technique that might just click with modern customers if wrapped in a new package.

Think of the comeback of newsletters. For a while, email was considered dead. But now? Indie creators are building empires off Substack and ConvertKit. Same channel, new soul.

Or imagine you're a toy startup. You find an obscure '90s Japanese board game that never caught on in the U.S. You localize it, update the design, launch a limited retro drop—and sell out in two days. That's not luck. That's knowing how to borrow the past to serve the present.

Practice Scenarios: Apply the Stratagem

Scenario 1: The Dead Format

You're in edtech, and discover that workbooks—yes, printed ones—are trending again with homeschoolers.

Your Challenge: How could you reintroduce this old format with a twist that fits your brand or product line?

Scenario 2: The Forgotten Feature

Your app has an old feature nobody uses—but it aligns perfectly with a current trend.

Your Challenge: How might you reposition or rename it so people see it in a whole new light?

Scenario 3: The Abandoned Idea

You scrapped a product concept last year due to low interest—but now, you're seeing buzz around similar tools.

Your Challenge: Could you resurrect that idea with fresh messaging, a new niche, or improved timing?

調虎離山

15. Lure the Tiger Out of the Mountain

Core Idea

This stratagem is about drawing a powerful opponent out of their stronghold or comfort zone—into a position where they are more vulnerable and easier to defeat.

Just like a tiger is dangerous in the mountains where it holds the advantage, you don't attack head-on.

Instead, you lure it down into the open where you can fight on your terms.

It teaches that you don't confront power directly.

You outmaneuver it, using strategy to shift the environment in your favor.

Historical Example

During the Three Kingdoms period, the general Zhou Yu faced a formidable enemy: Cao Cao. Cao Cao had a powerful navy and land army gathered at the stronghold of Red Cliffs. Instead of attacking directly, Zhou Yu used tactics to divide Cao Cao's forces, exploiting his unfamiliarity with river warfare and luring him into a naval engagement on terrain Zhou Yu had prepared. The result? Cao Cao's overwhelming advantage was neutralized, and his fleet was destroyed.

The tiger—Cao Cao—was pulled out of the mountains and defeated on unfamiliar ground.

Modern Marketing Scenario

Sometimes your biggest competitor—or your customer's attention—is entrenched. Instead of confronting them head-on, move the battle to a terrain where you have the advantage.

This stratagem is about shifting the context. Don't fight for visibility where your rival is strongest. Find a new playing field where their power means less... or where they might not even show up.

Say you're a small skincare brand competing with giants on Instagram. Instead of fighting in the same ad-heavy arena, you partner with niche hiking influencers on TikTok. "Trail-tested skin recovery kits" reach outdoor-loving customers who aren't being bombarded with skincare ads—and who care more about real results than glossy perfection.

Or you're launching a productivity app. Rather than targeting tech-savvy users already loyal to big names, you shift to college counseling offices and offer tailored features for academic coaching. Now you're not competing on features—you're offering solutions in a space where no one else is looking.

Practice Scenarios: Apply the Stratagem

Scenario 1: The Untouched Channel

Your competitor dominates Google Ads, but you've noticed they barely touch Reddit or podcasts.

Your Challenge: How can you craft a campaign that speaks to a different kind of audience in a less-contested space?

Scenario 2: The Relocated Offer

Your product isn't gaining traction on your website—but your users spend time on Discord.

Your Challenge: What would it look like to move your offer to where the conversation is already happening?

Scenario 3: The Reframed Problem

You're struggling to win clients in a saturated design market.

Your Challenge: Could you shift from selling "graphic design" to "branding for indie food trucks" and make the category your own?

欲擒故縱

16. Let the Enemy Go to Catch Them Later

Core Idea

This stratagem suggests that sometimes you must allow your opponent a temporary escape in order to trap them more effectively later. By feigning weakness or letting them flee, you lull them into overconfidence or into revealing their next move. In strategy, timing is everything—and patience can be your most powerful weapon.

Rather than striking immediately, you create the illusion of mercy, fatigue, or oversight. Your opponent relaxes, thinking they've escaped danger. But in truth, you've only loosened the leash—so when the moment is right, you tighten it again with devastating accuracy.

This stratagem teaches us to think long-term. Sometimes, letting go is not surrender—it's setting the stage for a more complete and decisive victory.

Historical Example

During the Three Kingdoms period, the general Lü Meng once pretended to retreat and abandon a strategic position to trick his rival Guan Yu. Guan Yu believed he had gained an advantage and pushed forward, leaving his rear exposed.

Lü Meng then launched a surprise attack on Guan Yu's base, cutting off his supplies and effectively ending his campaign.

What appeared to be surrender was actually a calculated bait—an invitation to overextend and fall into a trap.

Modern Marketing Scenario

Sometimes, the way to win a customer... is to stop trying so hard to win them.

Modern audiences are suspicious of aggressive marketing. They don't want to be pushed—they want to pull the value toward themselves. This stratagem taps into the power of restraint: giving just enough to spark interest, then stepping back to let curiosity grow.

Think of how some indie brands build mystique. A limited-time drop that's only announced via secret email list. A landing page that offers a free, incomplete tool—enough to hook the user, but not enough to solve the whole problem. Want more? You'll have to sign up, subscribe, or dive deeper.

Even in SaaS: a freemium model that's actually generous can create trust. When users aren't pressured to upgrade immediately, they often choose to want more—and convert later.

Practice Scenarios: Apply the Stratagem

Scenario 1: The Generous Freebie

You offer a free tool that solves 80% of a customer's problem, but leaves out the final step.

Your Challenge: How could you design that missing piece to be so valuable that users want to pay for it?

Scenario 2: The Pull-Back Campaign

You've been running a retargeting campaign that's burning budget without much return.

Your Challenge: What if you paused ads for a week and instead dropped an organic teaser campaign to build desire?

Scenario 3: The Limited Access Beta

Your product is ready, but instead of opening signups to everyone, you launch an invite-only beta.

Your Challenge: How can you use scarcity and curiosity to build demand before full launch?

抛磚引玉

17. Throw a Brick to Attract Jade

Core Idea

This stratagem is about using something of lesser value to draw out something more valuable from others. The "brick" represents an initial offer—an idea, opportunity, or gesture— that is intentionally modest but strategic. When offered wisely, it encourages others to respond with something greater—the "jade."

At its heart, this is a strategy of baiting: giving something small to spark a bigger return. But it's not always manipulative. It can be a form of generosity or investment— showing value first so others feel compelled to reciprocate.

It's a powerful move when trying to gain insight, win favor, or spark collaboration.

Historical Example

During the Tang Dynasty, the famous poet Wang Bo sought recognition at court. Instead of making direct requests, he sent a scroll of poetry—his "brick"—to a well-known scholar.

Impressed, the scholar shared Wang's work with the emperor, opening doors for the young writer.

The humble gesture sparked an outcome far beyond its immediate value—proof that a well-placed "brick" can draw out rare "jade."

Modern Marketing Scenario

You don't always need to have all the answers—you just need to offer something intriguing enough that others respond with something better.

In marketing, this is the principle of initiating value to invite even greater value in return. Share a free template, toolkit, or mini-course. Ask a provocative question that draws insightful replies. Start with a "brick"—simple, lightweight, not perfect. But if it's clever or useful enough, it brings the "jade" back: user feedback, media attention, collaboration requests, or even viral growth.

For example, a new analytics startup posts a free dashboard template for Notion users. It's basic—but the community response is huge. Soon, users start improving it, sharing ideas, and subscribing to the startup's newsletter. That one free template became their biggest lead magnet.

Or imagine a solo game designer releasing an open-source prototype on itch.io. The "brick" invites game dev YouTubers to playtest it, offer feedback, and—unprompted—start promoting it to niche audiences.

Practice Scenarios: Apply the Stratagem

Scenario 1: The "Starter Kit" Giveaway

You want to build email leads for your niche newsletter.

Your Challenge: What could you give away—a checklist, mini-ebook, resource vault—that's so useful people want to share it?

Scenario 2: The Incomplete Resource

You create a basic design tool, knowing it only scratches the surface.

Your Challenge: How can you make it open enough to let users modify, improve, and feel like co-creators?

Scenario 3: The Provocative Prompt

You run a coaching business and want to increase your social reach.

Your Challenge: What thought-provoking, unfinished idea or question could you post to attract deeper responses and spark conversation?

擒賊擒王

18. Capture the Ringleader to Capture the Gang

Core Idea

This stratagem teaches that in a group, the leader is the key. If you want to dismantle a team, a faction, or even a movement—go after its central figure. Taking down the leader often causes confusion and disunity among their followers, making resistance easier to overcome.

The logic is simple: cut off the head, and the body falls apart. This strategy works not just through force but through persuasion, negotiation, or manipulation aimed directly at the core influencer or authority figure.

This tactic is especially useful when confronting a complex or hostile organization. Instead of fighting every part, you target the command center.

Historical Example

During the early Han Dynasty, Emperor Gaozu (Liu Bang) faced ongoing rebellion from a powerful warlord named Chen Xi.

Instead of confronting the rebel forces head-on, Liu Bang used intelligence and spies to locate and eliminate Chen Xi directly. Once the leader was gone, the rebellion swiftly collapsed.

By capturing—or neutralizing—the core leader, Liu Bang ended what could have been a prolonged conflict with minimal loss.

Modern Marketing Scenario

Sometimes, the key to winning a market isn't to chase every potential customer—it's to win over the right one.

This stratagem is about identifying the key decision-maker, trendsetter, or high-leverage channel that influences many others. If you convert them, others will follow.

Think about how certain products go viral not through paid ads, but through a single influential figure. A parenting app gets picked up by a popular "momfluencer." A productivity tool is featured by a top YouTube reviewer. A fitness brand wins over the local gym owner—and suddenly, their entire client base follows.

Even in B2B marketing, this shows up in the form of strategic enterprise sales. Rather than trying to win over everyone in a company, you target the head of operations. Win her trust, and she brings your product to her entire department.

Practice Scenarios: Apply the Stratagem

Scenario 1: The Influencer Key

You run a niche skincare brand with limited reach.

Your Challenge: Instead of broad marketing, can you identify one micro-influencer whose endorsement would lead their whole audience to try your product?

Scenario 2: The Gatekeeper in B2B

You sell a team-based project management tool.

Your Challenge: Who's the "kingpin" role in your client orgs—someone whose approval could unlock full-team adoption?

Scenario 3: The Trendsetting Customer

You run a small café in a college town.

Your Challenge: Is there a specific student group, club, or professor whose presence or endorsement could draw in the rest?

混戰計

PART 4: Chaos Stratagems
Strategies to exploit confusion or disruption

釜底抽薪

19. Remove the firewood from under the pot

Core Idea

When a situation seems intense or a rival appears formidable, it's often tempting to confront them head-on. However, this stratagem urges a subtler approach: target the source of their strength rather than the strength itself. Like removing the firewood beneath a boiling pot, you don't fight the flames—you eliminate the fuel.

This method is not only more efficient, but also less risky. By undermining an opponent's foundation—be it resources, alliances, morale, or public support—you can diffuse the danger without direct conflict.

It's a lesson in focusing your efforts where they have the most leverage.

Historical Example

In the Spring and Autumn period, the famous general Wu Zixu helped King Helü of Wu wage war against the neighboring state of Chu. Instead of clashing with Chu's powerful army outright, Wu Zixu advised attacking the capital's water supply and cutting off reinforcements. Without a steady source of water and support, the formidable Chu defenses quickly crumbled, leading to a decisive Wu victory.

This wasn't a battle of brute strength. It was a calculated dismantling of the enemy's foundation. The strategy didn't require outmatching the opponent—it simply required outthinking them.

Modern Marketing Scenario

In business, it's easy to focus on fighting competitors head-on—launching features to match theirs, running ads to win back customers, or lowering prices to compete. But sometimes, it's far more effective to quietly weaken what's fueling their success.

This stratagem is about cutting off the oxygen, not the fire. Say a competitor is dominating search traffic in your niche thanks to a popular affiliate network. Rather than outranking them directly, you launch a campaign to recruit those same affiliates with higher commissions, better conversion rates, or exclusive early access to new products. Within weeks, their biggest traffic sources begin to dry up. Or imagine a rival SaaS tool is thriving because it integrates with a specific workflow platform. You build a free browser extension that dramatically improves that workflow—without needing the original tool. You're not fighting them—you're removing the reason people needed them in the first place.

This isn't sabotage. It's strategic subtraction. Don't exhaust yourself attacking the flames. Go after the fuel source—and watch the fire go out on its own.

Practice Scenarios: Apply the Stratagem

Scenario 1: The Influencer Supply Chain

A competitor is getting tons of traffic from creators who promote them in tutorials.

Your Challenge: What alternative could you offer those same creators—like better referral tools, premium support, or co-branded content—that would quietly shift their loyalty?

Scenario 2: The Dependency Play

A rival product relies on a third-party API or integration that users love.

Your Challenge: Could you create a simpler or more direct experience that bypasses that dependency—and subtly position your tool as the faster, cleaner alternative?

Scenario 3: The Support Drain

A well-funded startup is winning with aggressive customer acquisition, but their support team is visibly overwhelmed.

Your Challenge: How might you focus your messaging on peace-of-mind, fast response times, or human support—drawing away frustrated users while their churn problem grows?

混水摸魚

20. Fish in Troubled Waters

Core Idea

When the world is in disorder, opportunities often hide beneath the surface. "Fishing in troubled waters" means taking advantage of chaos, confusion, or instability—not by causing it, but by remaining calm, observant, and ready to act.

Like an angler who casts their net when the water is stirred and fish can't see clearly, a strategist knows when to strike while others are distracted, arguing, or paralyzed by uncertainty.

This strategy requires patience and a sharp eye for timing. It's not about being unethical—it's about spotting neglected chances and moving decisively while others hesitate. In uncertain times, power often shifts quietly into the hands of those who remain steady and opportunistic.

Historical Example

During the decline of the Qin dynasty, widespread rebellions erupted across the empire. Liu Bang, the future founder of the Han dynasty, was originally a minor official. Amid the chaos of collapsing authority and fighting warlords, he quietly built his own following.

While stronger generals clashed and weakened each other, Liu Bang focused on gaining the trust of local people, expanding his forces, and seizing key territories without engaging in major battles. He ultimately unified the land by "fishing in troubled waters."

Modern Marketing Scenario

When markets get messy, most brands get nervous. But this stratagem reminds us: chaos isn't always bad—it's camouflage. When no one knows what's going on, your boldest moves often go unnoticed... until they work.

This is about timing your actions during turbulence—industry shifts, platform meltdowns, or even cultural noise. While others freeze or panic, you move decisively and quietly gain ground.

Imagine a wave of AI tools flooding the market, confusing users with wild promises. Instead of rushing to stand out, you quietly release a humble, well-explained alternative—positioned as "the calm in the storm." Or when a social media platform is facing backlash over new policies, you launch a creator-friendly community space and invite frustrated users to test it out.

It's not opportunism in a negative sense—it's strategic awareness. While everyone's busy fighting the storm, you're fishing—steady hands, clear goals, and a net ready for the right moment.

Practice Scenarios: Apply the Stratagem

Scenario 1: The Platform Shakeup

A major platform in your industry just changed its algorithm, and creators are in chaos.

Your Challenge: What simple resource—like a survival guide, analytics tool, or migration checklist—could you launch right now to attract attention and build trust?

Scenario 2: The Competitor Collapse

A well-known startup is laying off staff and scaling back its roadmap.

Your Challenge: How might you quietly connect with their user base—through retargeting, side-by-side comparison pages, or migration assistance—while they're still reeling?

Scenario 3: The Cultural Disruption

A global event or controversy has left your audience uncertain and distracted.

Your Challenge: Could you pivot your messaging to offer stability, clarity, or emotional resonance—becoming a trusted voice while others stay silent or scramble?

金蟬脫殼

21. The Cicada Sheds Its Shell

Core Idea

This stratagem is about creating an illusion while making a clean exit. Just as a cicada leaves behind its empty shell clinging to a tree, you leave behind a convincing facade while quietly removing yourself from danger or responsibility. It's a strategy of withdrawal disguised as continuity.

Rather than resisting head-on, you preserve your strength by slipping away unnoticed. You give others something to focus on—a project that looks busy, a communication that sounds confident—while your true action happens elsewhere. In both warfare and the workplace, this strategy buys you time, distance, and clarity.

This is especially useful when the situation is hostile, chaotic, or politically dangerous. You don't confront the pressure directly—you vanish from its grasp while leaving a version of yourself behind to absorb the fallout.

Historical Example

During the Three Kingdoms period in China, the warlord Sun Quan once feigned a full-scale naval buildup along the Yangtze River, convincing his rival Cao Cao that a major attack was coming. In reality, Sun Quan quietly relocated his fleet and troops to another target. By the time Cao Cao discovered the truth, the original threat was just an empty "shell"—the real action had already shifted.

This stratagem allowed Sun Quan to preserve his forces and catch his enemy off guard, all while projecting strength.

Modern Marketing Scenario

Sometimes, the smartest move isn't to confront a failing situation—it's to quietly exit while leaving behind a version of yourself that looks like everything's still fine. This stratagem is about strategic withdrawal wrapped in illusion. In business, that might mean phasing out a project, brand, or product line—but doing it in a way that preserves reputation, avoids panic, and buys time for your next move.

Imagine a founder whose first startup isn't gaining traction. Instead of announcing a shutdown, she "pauses" updates and shifts focus to a new open-source tool under her personal brand. Her old site stays live, looking functional. Investors and followers stay calm. Months later, she resurfaces with a new direction—and none of the public shame of failure. Or a SaaS company wants to exit a crowded vertical. They spin off the product, leave behind minimal support content, and redirect their internal focus to a more promising niche. Outwardly, it looks like continuity. Internally, it's a clean break.

This isn't deception—it's graceful disengagement. The shell you leave behind buys time, protects your brand, and lets you move where the real opportunity lies.

Practice Scenarios: Apply the Stratagem

Scenario 1: The Silent Sunset

You want to wind down a product that's no longer sustainable—but still has a few loyal users.

Your Challenge: How could you keep the site or tool semi-operational (e.g., open-source, community-run, or archived) while shifting your energy elsewhere?

Scenario 2: The Stealthy Pivot

Your brand identity is tied to a niche you no longer believe in.

Your Challenge: What "bridge content" or side project could you release that lets you gradually transition audiences without announcing a full pivot?

Scenario 3: The Founder Disappearance

You're burned out and need a break, but your audience expects constant presence.

Your Challenge: Could you pre-schedule content, repurpose archives, or launch a low-maintenance version of your offering that keeps the illusion of activity while you regroup?

關門捉賊

22. Lock the door to catch the thief

Core Idea

This stratagem centers on control and entrapment. Rather than chasing your opponent, you seal off all exits and wait for them to act. It's about anticipating the enemy's escape route and cutting it off before they even try to flee. The moment they reveal themselves, you strike.

The phrase evokes the image of a thief hiding in a house. Instead of rushing in and causing chaos, you quietly lock all the doors and windows—ensuring there's nowhere for the thief to run. Then, when the moment is right, you catch them cleanly and decisively.

It's a strategy that combines patience with precision. In the modern world, it's useful when you suspect someone is acting in bad faith, or when you want to expose the truth behind a façade. You don't attack directly—instead, you set up a trap that forces the other side to reveal themselves or make a mistake.

Historical Example

During the Three Kingdoms period in China, general Lü Meng used this strategy when attacking the city of Jiangling. Instead of charging into battle, he cut off all the city's supply lines and escape routes. Over time, the defenders realized they had no way out. Eventually, the city surrendered without Lü Meng needing to waste his forces on a risky assault.

Lü Meng's calm and calculated encirclement allowed him to win with minimal bloodshed—because he had "locked the door," and all the enemy could do was wait for capture.

Modern Marketing Scenario

Sometimes the best way to catch a threat isn't to chase it— it's to trap it. This stratagem is about control: anticipating bad actors, manipulative customers, or sneaky competitors—and setting up a system that forces them to reveal themselves. In modern marketing, this might mean tightening access, building in transparency tools, or creating systems that encourage self-selection. You're not attacking—you're creating an environment where the truth exposes itself. Let's say you suspect that a few users are abusing your free trial system to keep creating new accounts. Instead of launching into a crackdown, you revise your onboarding to include subtle verification steps and usage limits that only impact repeat abusers—while regular users glide through unaffected. You lock the doors—but only to those trying to sneak out. Or maybe you're running a community where someone keeps derailing discussions. You quietly shift moderation policies, implement audit trails, and publish clear standards. Soon, the disruptors reveal themselves—and now you can act with clear evidence and broad support. It's a strategy of quiet confidence. You don't panic. You prepare. And when the thief tries to run, the exit's already closed.

Practice Scenarios: Apply the Stratagem

Scenario 1: The Trial Abuser

You run a freemium SaaS product, but users are cycling through free trials using fake emails.

Your Challenge: How could you redesign the sign-up flow or value delivery to make repeated abuse obvious—and unattractive—without hurting honest users?

Scenario 2: The Community Saboteur

Your online group has a member spreading negativity in subtle ways, but they haven't broken any rules—yet.

Your Challenge: What changes could you make to discussion guidelines, reporting tools, or visibility settings to surface bad behavior and isolate the impact?

Scenario 3: The Quiet Competitor

You suspect a competitor is posing as a "customer" to gather intel.

Your Challenge: Could you create a controlled funnel—like a gated beta or onboarding quiz—that helps you track unusual behavior patterns and flag suspicious accounts?

遠交近攻

23. Befriend the distant, attack the nearby

Core Idea

This stratagem recommends forming alliances with distant powers while targeting those closer to you. The logic is geographical and strategic: nearby enemies pose an immediate threat and are easier to strike, while distant powers can be partners—at least temporarily—because they do not compete for the same territory or influence.

In essence, it's about managing your energy and risk by eliminating threats that are within reach and securing your rear by avoiding conflicts on multiple fronts. It's also about using diplomacy as a weapon: forming friendships not necessarily out of trust, but out of strategic interest.

It's a classic divide-and-conquer method: isolate the target, build temporary cooperation elsewhere, and take down adversaries step by step.

Historical Example

During the Warring States period in ancient China, the state of Qin used this stratagem effectively. Qin would make diplomatic pacts with distant states, sometimes even offering gifts or marriage alliances, while focusing military efforts on its immediate neighbors like Han and Wei.

By reducing threats one by one from the inside out, and delaying conflict with stronger, distant states, Qin steadily expanded its territory. Eventually, it turned on its distant "friends" after growing strong enough, completing its conquest of the other six states and unifying China.

Modern Marketing Scenario

In business, we often think our biggest threat is the loudest competitor on the other side of the internet. But sometimes, it's the ones right next to us—offering similar products, targeting the same audience, fighting for the same keywords. This stratagem teaches us to form alliances with distant players—even those in the same industry—while focusing competitive energy on nearby threats. Imagine you're building a niche task management app. Instead of competing with massive platforms like Notion or Asana, you integrate with them. You highlight your tool as a focused companion product, earning mentions in their communities. Meanwhile, you outmaneuver other small tools that are trying to stand alone. Or you're launching a local brand in the food space. Instead of competing with faraway DTC brands, you partner with them for giveaways or cross-promotions—building social proof. But down the street, a similar business is your real threat. You double down on customer service, neighborhood events, and local SEO—winning the ground game. It's not about betrayal. It's strategic positioning. You shake hands with the faraway giants, and quietly win the battles happening in your backyard.

Practice Scenarios: Apply the Stratagem

Scenario 1: The Unlikely Partner

You run a fitness app, and a massive wellness platform shares a portion of your target audience.

Your Challenge: How might you pitch a collaboration that makes you look complementary—not competitive—while you focus on taking market share from closer rivals?

Scenario 2: The Local Land Grab

You're a new café in a city full of trendy chains.

Your Challenge: Could you partner with an international bean supplier or global artist community for buzz—while building irresistible offers that pull in local foot traffic?

Scenario 3: The Category Clutter

You've launched a new marketing podcast, and there are hundreds like it.

Your Challenge: What niche influencers or global thought leaders could you invite to guest—while using those appearances to gain credibility and pull listeners away from competing shows in your exact format?

假道伐虢

24. Attack a neighbor by passing through another

Core Idea

This stratagem is about exploiting access or cooperation under false pretenses. It suggests pretending to peacefully pass through an ally or neutral territory while secretly planning to strike a third party. In broader terms, it's a tactic of deception—using an apparent objective to mask your real one. The metaphor comes from ancient military campaigns: a general asks permission to march troops through a friendly state to attack a distant enemy but instead turns and conquers the helpful state itself.

In the workplace, it means using alliances or stated goals to achieve hidden objectives. It's not always malicious—it could involve working with others to get close to decision-makers, influence a situation indirectly, or gain access to restricted opportunities. This is a strategy of misdirection and opportunism. It teaches that even "cooperation" can be weaponized when intentions are masked.

Historical Example

During the Spring and Autumn period of Chinese history, the state of Jin wanted to attack the state of Guo but needed to pass through the smaller state of Yu. Jin requested safe passage, claiming it was only moving troops to a distant border. Yu agreed. But once Jin's army was inside Yu's territory, it turned and attacked Yu instead—then moved on to take Guo as well.

The stratagem worked because Yu believed Jin's stated intention. Jin exploited the openness of one to defeat both.

Modern Marketing Scenario

Sometimes the fastest way to your real goal is through a detour. This stratagem is about masking your true target with a decoy mission—entering one space, only to strike in another.

In marketing, this can mean positioning your brand as serving one purpose while quietly capturing another, more strategic opportunity. You "pass through" a visible market to gain access to a hidden one.

Imagine you're building a customer support tool, but instead of competing directly with Zendesk or Intercom, you release a simple "employee feedback" platform. It's light, unthreatening, and gets you embedded in internal HR systems. Once inside, you expand features—and now you're handling customer support too. Or a small design agency offers "free branding audits" to nonprofits. It seems like charity work. But behind the scenes, you're building case studies, social proof, and relationships that help you land work with large corporate partners who respect your impact-focused portfolio. The key here isn't deception—it's direction. You take the path people let you through... then pivot to where the real value lies.

Practice Scenarios: Apply the Stratagem

Scenario 1: The Trojan Tool

You're building a workplace productivity suite, but IT teams are a tough gatekeeper.

Your Challenge: What smaller utility—like a calendar overlay or meeting note plugin—could you offer to slip into teams first, and later expand your presence?

Scenario 2: The Portfolio in Disguise

You're trying to break into luxury product photography, but high-end clients don't return your emails.

Your Challenge: Could you shoot free work for niche startups with beautiful branding, then showcase those shots in a premium-style portfolio that gets noticed?

Scenario 3: The Conference Detour

You can't afford a booth at a major tech event—but there's a side event for student founders.

Your Challenge: How could you show up with a valuable resource, giveaway, or workshop that gets you into the right rooms—even if it's not your "official" audience?

並戰計

PART 5: Alliance Stratagems
Strategies for diplomacy, alliances,
and indirect power moves

偷樑換柱

25. Steal the beams and replace them with rotten timbers

Core Idea

This stratagem is about gradual substitution—replacing something strong, valuable, or central with something weaker or more controllable, without drawing attention. It's not a frontal assault. Instead, it erodes the foundation of strength so subtly that by the time collapse happens, it's too late to fix.

The metaphor comes from construction: imagine replacing the key support beams in a house with rotten ones while the owner isn't watching. Eventually, the house collapses—not because of an attack, but because its very structure was undermined.

In modern terms, this applies to power structures, systems, teams, or even ideas. If you can't confront the strength directly, you weaken it by reshaping its internal elements. Often used over time, this tactic thrives on deception, patience, and careful planning.

Historical Example

During the Three Kingdoms period, the brilliant strategist Lü Meng sought to conquer Jing Province, which was under the control of the famous general Guan Yu. Rather than attacking outright, Lü Meng convinced his leader, Sun Quan, to first replace Guan Yu's loyal commanders with officers loyal to Wu—under the guise of cooperation and peace.

Over time, Jing Province's defense was hollowed out from the inside. When Sun Quan finally launched his attack, Guan Yu found himself surrounded by unfamiliar and unreliable allies. The territory fell swiftly—because the beams had already been swapped.

Modern Marketing Scenario

Sometimes, you don't need to tear down a competitor—you just need to weaken their foundation, quietly and over time. This stratagem is about subtle replacement: identifying what's holding up someone else's success... and swapping it out with something less stable, or more favorable to you.

In business, this might mean shifting loyalty. Replacing trust. Swapping out habits. All without raising alarms.

Let's say a competitor dominates your niche thanks to a massive affiliate program. You don't attack them—you build quiet relationships with their top affiliates, offering higher payouts or more flexible terms. Over time, their support structure weakens... and collapses.

Or imagine a popular newsletter relies on a single content curation tool. You launch a smoother, cheaper alternative— then reach out to power users with migration support and early access perks. Slowly, the ecosystem tilts your way.

This isn't about sabotage. It's about evolution. When someone builds their empire on borrowed beams, all you have to do is offer replacements—and wait for gravity to do the rest.

Practice Scenarios: Apply the Stratagem

Scenario 1: The Channel Swap

Your competitor relies heavily on a specific influencer agency to generate leads.

Your Challenge: How could you quietly attract those same influencers with better onboarding, higher transparency, or more creative freedom?

Scenario 2: The Platform Undermining

A rival's product runs on a clunky third-party integration that frustrates users, but everyone's used to it.

Your Challenge: Could you build a native experience so intuitive that users naturally advocate for switching—even before your rival catches on?

Scenario 3: The Content Crumble

An industry blog earns SEO dominance by reposting user-generated templates.

Your Challenge: What if you launched a template-sharing community with better UX, clearer attribution, and creator rewards—pulling their contributors (and search traffic) away over time?

指桑罵槐

26. Point at the mulberry tree but curse the locust tree

Core Idea

This stratagem is about indirect criticism or warning. Instead of confronting someone directly, you deliver your message to a third party—knowing the real target will understand the implication. It's a subtle but effective tactic, often used to avoid direct conflict or preserve social harmony while still expressing dissatisfaction or asserting authority.

The phrase comes from traditional storytelling: a person scolds someone else by pretending to scold another. For example, a parent might yell at a neighbor's child in front of their own, with the real message meant for the child listening nearby. It's about maintaining face, sending a warning, or influencing behavior without open confrontation.

This strategy is especially useful in hierarchical or politically sensitive environments. It allows the speaker to make a point without direct accusation—providing room for interpretation, plausible deniability, or diplomacy.

Historical Example

During the Han Dynasty, Emperor Wu was displeased with a certain general's conduct but did not want to cause public embarrassment or backlash. So instead, he delivered a strong rebuke to another, lower-ranking official for a similar offense—knowing that the general would understand the message was actually meant for him.

By "pointing at the mulberry tree and cursing the locust tree," the emperor controlled the message without sparking direct confrontation or rebellion. It was a way of issuing a warning and exerting control through indirect means.

Modern Marketing Scenario

Not every message has to be direct to hit its mark. This stratagem is about saying one thing... so the right person hears another. When confrontation would cause backlash—or when subtlety works better—indirect communication becomes a powerful tool. In modern marketing, this shows up when you address a problem "in general," but the real audience knows you're talking to (or about) them. Imagine you run a brand that prides itself on ethical sourcing, and a competitor has just been called out for questionable labor practices. Instead of naming names, you publish a blog post titled "What Fair Trade Really Means in 2025"—with transparency checklists, supplier photos, and customer testimonials. You point at the mulberry tree... but everyone hears the message loud and clear. Or you're launching a course for creators frustrated by algorithm changes. You don't rant about platforms—you share "5 ways creators are reclaiming their audience" and highlight success stories from people who moved to email lists or communities. Subtle, but sharp. This isn't passive-aggressive. It's strategic storytelling. When your point is too important to ignore—but too risky to say outright—let the metaphor do the work.

Practice Scenarios: Apply the Stratagem

Scenario 1: The Quiet Clapback

A competitor recently copied your product but positioned it as "the original."

Your Challenge: How might you publish a piece that tells your origin story with dates, milestones, and customer love—without ever mentioning the imitator?

Scenario 2: The Unspoken Rebuke

An influencer in your niche spreads misinformation, and your audience is getting confused.

Your Challenge: Could you create a fact-based resource, comparison chart, or short video that calmly lays out the truth—without starting a war?

Scenario 3: The Policy Pivot

You're rolling out a new feature because of platform changes, but don't want to sound reactive.

Your Challenge: How might you announce it in a way that positions you as proactive and thoughtful—while those who know the real backstory catch the deeper meaning?

假痴不顛

27. Feign ignorance without going mad

Core Idea

This stratagem encourages pretending to be foolish or uninformed—without actually losing control or credibility. It's a delicate act: you appear harmless, inattentive, or even incompetent, but you're quietly observing, analyzing, and preparing to act.

This approach disarms others. They may underestimate you, lower their defenses, or even reveal intentions they wouldn't share with someone they see as a threat. By feigning ignorance, you can hide your true strengths and intentions until the time is right.

The key is balance. You must seem genuinely disengaged, but in truth, you stay alert and strategic. This is not about giving up control—it's about controlling what others think you understand.

Historical Example

During the Three Kingdoms period, Zhuge Liang—one of the most revered strategists in Chinese history—once deliberately acted dim-witted when visiting the Wu kingdom. In front of rival officials, he played the role of an absent-minded guest, avoiding serious political discussion. But behind the scenes, he was gathering intelligence, studying personalities, and quietly negotiating with the Wu ruler. His "foolishness" put everyone at ease and allowed him to operate without suspicion. Once he had the alliances he needed, he dropped the act and emerged as a powerful political force. Zhuge Liang's success came from his ability to hide brilliance behind a mask of simplicity.

Modern Marketing Scenario

Sometimes, the smartest person in the room is the one who pretends not to be. This stratagem is about strategic underestimation—intentionally appearing passive, harmless, or out of the loop... so you can observe, gather intel, or avoid early resistance.

In business, this might mean letting others believe you're not a threat, not ready, or not even aware—until it's too late for them to react. Imagine you're quietly building a new platform that will compete with a dominant player in your space. Instead of teasing features or promising a revolution, you post soft, self-deprecating updates like "Still learning... building one line of code at a time." The incumbents don't notice you. But when you launch? You've already built everything—and the early adopters are ready. Or you're at an industry event where everyone's boasting about numbers and scale. You don't correct them when they assume you're just starting out. You ask questions. You let them talk. You learn everything. Feigning ignorance isn't about lying. It's about choosing when to reveal your cards—and how much power silence can hold.

Practice Scenarios: Apply the Stratagem

Scenario 1: The Undercover Builder

You're developing a product that could disrupt a stagnant space—but competitors are watching closely.

Your Challenge: How might you share your journey in a way that appears casual or incomplete, while building your waitlist and gathering feedback quietly?

Scenario 2: The Power Listener

You're networking at events full of ego and noise.

Your Challenge: What prompts, questions, or naive-sounding comments could help others let their guard down—so you gain valuable insights without giving away your own plans?

Scenario 3: The "Beginner" Thread

You're an expert, but your audience loves raw, relatable content.

Your Challenge: Could you write a social post or email like "Things I still don't get about marketing..." that invites connection, shares truth, and hides the fact that you're 10 steps ahead?

上屋抽梯

28. Climb the roof and pull up the ladder

Core Idea

This stratagem is about deliberately cutting off retreat—both for yourself and others. Once someone is committed to a course of action, you remove the option of backing out. It forces full commitment, whether for strategic momentum or manipulation. The image is vivid: you convince someone to climb to the roof with you—then remove the ladder. They can't go back. Now they must continue forward, for better or worse. It can be used to trap enemies or push allies to act boldly without hesitation. In business and leadership, this tactic can appear as a point-of-no-return maneuver. You create a situation where someone must commit—whether by limiting their choices, using deadlines, or escalating their involvement past the point of reversal. It's a powerful tactic, but also risky. Used with care, it creates focus and urgency. Used deceptively, it can break trust. Either way, it reflects the idea: once you're up high, there's no way down except forward.

Historical Example

During the Ming Dynasty, General Qi Jiguang used this stratagem when training undisciplined troops. He once ordered his soldiers to climb a narrow cliff path for a surprise attack on pirates. After they ascended, he had the ladders pulled up behind them.

With no retreat possible, the only option was to press forward and fight. The soldiers, knowing they couldn't flee, fought with greater determination and won the battle.

Qi used this method repeatedly—not just to trap enemies, but to steel the resolve of his own men. When there's no safe way back, even the hesitant find courage.

Modern Marketing Scenario

Commitment changes everything—especially when there's no way back. This stratagem is about removing the escape route, either for yourself or others, so forward motion becomes the only option.

In marketing and product strategy, this often means engineering a point of no return—forcing bold action, high engagement, or customer conversion by removing the option to hesitate or backtrack.

Imagine you're launching a new course and want people to actually finish it. Instead of offering perpetual access, you limit it to a 30-day cohort with accountability groups, no refunds, and a shared leaderboard. Once someone joins, the "ladder" disappears. They're on the roof—and it's go time. Or your startup has been tinkering with soft launches and MVPs for months. You finally announce a live countdown to Product Hunt launch day, alert your list, and promise an AMA the next morning. Now you have to ship. There's no climbing down.

This strategy works because most people avoid discomfort. But when the only direction is forward, even reluctant players start to run.

Practice Scenarios: Apply the Stratagem

Scenario 1: The Strategic Guest Spot

You're trying to grow your audience but have zero followers.

Your Challenge: What podcast, newsletter, or YouTube channel already serves your ideal audience—and how might you offer them something valuable enough to earn a feature?

Scenario 2: The API Advantage

You've built a tool that works beautifully with a bigger platform.

Your Challenge: How could you showcase that relationship— through integrations, case studies, or tutorial content—so users of that platform discover and trust you faster?

Scenario 3: The Community Climb

You run a niche service, but your dream customers all hang out in someone else's Discord.

Your Challenge: Could you become an active, helpful contributor in that space—and slowly build a reputation without ever sounding like you're selling?

反客為主

30. Turn the Guest into the Host

Core Idea

This stratagem centers on the idea of reversing roles to gain control. Originally, it referred to a guest or outsider gradually taking over the position and power of the host. In modern terms, it's about subtly shifting influence or ownership, especially when you begin from a weaker or outsider position.

At its core, this is a strategy of infiltration followed by domination. Rather than confronting power head-on, you integrate into the system and slowly redirect its control to yourself. This can happen through persistent presence, winning trust, or demonstrating superior competence—until others begin to rely on you more than they realize.

It's not necessarily manipulative; sometimes, this stratagem simply reflects what happens when someone steps up and proves themselves indispensable.

Historical Example

During the Warring States period, General Tian Dan of Qi devised a clever ruse after losing his homeland to Yan.

While posing as a refugee among the local population, he gradually gained their trust. By offering small strategies and helping organize defense efforts, he rose in influence.

Eventually, he was entrusted with command and led a successful campaign to reclaim Qi territory. Though he started as a guest among strangers, he became the de facto leader—turning the guest into the host.

Modern Marketing Scenario

You might start as an outsider—but you don't have to stay that way. This stratagem is about gradually shifting from a passive role to one of control, influence, or ownership—until the people who once invited you in now rely on you to lead. In the modern marketing world, this shows up when you embed yourself so deeply into a community, tool, or ecosystem that you become essential. You're no longer just participating—you're steering.

Say you join a niche Slack group for indie makers. You start by asking questions, then answering a few. Eventually, you host a weekly "launch support" thread. A few months later, the admins make you a mod. Then? You spin off your own curated newsletter for that community. You started as a guest—but now you're setting the table. Or maybe you contribute to a major open-source project. Your PRs get merged. Your name gets recognized. You release an extension that becomes the go-to for users. Suddenly, you're the one shaping the direction, even if your name isn't on the homepage. This isn't a hostile takeover. It's earned leadership. You build value, trust, and presence—until the house is, in part, yours.

Practice Scenarios: Apply the Stratagem

Scenario 1: The Community Steward

You're active in a niche forum or Discord but want to become more visible.

Your Challenge: What recurring value—like summaries, roundups, or challenges—could you offer that makes people look to you even more than the original mods?

Scenario 2: The Integrator's Ascent

You've built a small plugin for a larger platform and want to grow your influence.

Your Challenge: How might you build onboarding guides, video tutorials, or even host office hours that position you as the go-to expert for new users?

Scenario 3: The Partner Pivot

You're contributing guest content to a bigger brand's blog.

Your Challenge: Could you propose a co-branded initiative, course, or product bundle that quietly shifts the spotlight toward your offering—without triggering resistance?

敗戰計

PART 6: Desperate Stratagems
Strategies for crisis, retreat, or comeback

美人計

31. The beauty trap

Core Idea

This stratagem involves using attraction, desire, or emotional entanglement as a weapon. Originally, it referred to sending beautiful people to seduce an enemy, causing them to lose focus, make poor decisions, or fight among themselves. Today, it's more broadly about using charm, distraction, or allure—of any kind—to gain strategic advantage.

The core principle is psychological manipulation: when logic fails, emotions can be exploited. Whether it's vanity, romance, admiration, or lust, the beauty trap draws people in through their desires and blinds them to the consequences.

This is not necessarily about literal beauty. In the workplace, the "trap" might be flattery, exclusive attention, or offering someone a role they find too tempting to resist—only to influence their decisions or distract them from other priorities. It's a powerful but ethically risky tool.

Historical Example

In ancient China, during the Warring States period, the state of Wu sent two renowned beauties, Xi Shi and Zheng Dan, to the court of the King of Yue.

The king became obsessed, neglected his duties, and lost the support of his ministers. As a result, his kingdom weakened, and Wu eventually took advantage of the situation to launch a successful attack.

The strategy wasn't just about romance—it was psychological warfare disguised as pleasure.

Modern Marketing Scenario

Not all traps are built with threats—some are made of charm. This stratagem is about using attraction, allure, or irresistible appeal to disarm your target before they even realize they've let their guard down. In modern marketing, that "beauty" might be stunning design, a magnetic personality, a luxurious unboxing experience, or even a romanticized brand story. Whatever form it takes, its purpose is the same: win attention, weaken defenses, and make the logical mind take a back seat. Imagine you're launching a premium productivity app. Instead of focusing on features, you tell the story of a burned-out founder rebuilding their life, and back it with breathtaking visuals and calming sounds. It's not just an app—it's a lifestyle fantasy. People sign up because they're pulled in emotionally. They stay for the actual utility. Or you're a bootstrapped skincare brand. Competing on ingredients is a losing game. So you wrap your product in vintage-style packaging, shoot moody cinematic ads, and position it as a hidden gem from another era. The story sells before anyone checks the label. The "beauty" isn't the value— it's the invitation. Once they step inside, you show them what's real.

Practice Scenarios: Apply the Stratagem

Scenario 1: The Emotional Hook

Your product solves a real problem, but users aren't clicking through.

Your Challenge: What visual story, aesthetic, or vibe could you wrap your messaging in to make the solution feel like a dream—not just a utility?

Scenario 2: The Seductive Freebie

You want to grow your email list but need something more magnetic than a PDF guide.

Your Challenge: Could you offer an experience—like an interactive quiz, "ritual kit," or behind-the-scenes narrative—that pulls people in through intrigue and mood?

Scenario 3: The Visual Trojan Horse

You're entering a crowded niche where everyone looks the same.

Your Challenge: How might you use color, typography, or visual storytelling to create a brand presence so striking that people click before they even know what you're offering?

空城計

32. The Empty Fort Strategy

Core Idea

This stratagem is about using boldness to mask weakness. When you're vulnerable but want to appear strong, the best defense may be a calm, confident show—so unnerving that your opponent suspects a trap.

It's a psychological tactic: if you're outnumbered or underprepared, acting like you've laid a trap might scare your enemies into retreating.

The more exposed you are, the more audacious your bluff must be.

This stratagem teaches us that confidence, when timed right, can be more powerful than actual strength. It works best when your opponent is cautious or prone to overthinking.

Historical Example

During the Three Kingdoms period, Zhuge Liang found himself in a city with no troops to defend it. Enemy general Sima Yi approached with a large army. Instead of fleeing or hiding, Zhuge Liang ordered the gates opened wide, had his men sweep the streets, and calmly played his zither from the city walls. Sima Yi, suspecting a hidden ambush, halted the attack and eventually retreated. Zhuge Liang's empty fort was a masterful bluff that worked because of his reputation for cunning.

It's a classic case of using the enemy's fear and assumptions against them.

Modern Marketing Scenario

When you're weak, act strong. When you have nothing, act like you planned it that way. This stratagem is about projecting unshakable confidence precisely when you're most vulnerable—so your opponent hesitates, second-guesses, or retreats altogether. In modern marketing, this might mean turning your lack of resources into an aesthetic. Flaunting your minimalism. Broadcasting your beta status with pride. Done right, it becomes a strength—one that makes others suspect you know something they don't. Imagine your product just launched and only has a few users. Instead of hiding that fact, you post: "We're keeping things intentionally small so we can obsess over each user's experience. Founding members get a direct line to the team." Suddenly, what looked like emptiness now feels exclusive. Or you're an indie game dev with no budget for ads. So you release a mysterious trailer with no voiceover, no explanation—just mood and mystery. It gets shared because people assume there's something deeper going on. The empty fort works when you've earned even a little trust. If your reputation is solid, a bold bluff isn't cowardice—it's strategy.

Practice Scenarios: Apply the Stratagem

Scenario 1: The Scarcity Flex

Your platform isn't scaling yet, and you only have a handful of users.

Your Challenge: How might you reframe that as a "private beta," "invite-only" phase, or "early access club" that makes people want in before the crowd arrives?

Scenario 2: The Confident Launch Page

You don't have product-market fit—but you still need to show up.

Your Challenge: Could you design a landing page so clean and focused that people assume there must be serious demand behind it?

Scenario 3: The Unavailable Offer

You're not ready to sell yet, but want to build intrigue.

Your Challenge: How might you use a waitlist, vague teaser, or cryptic social post to make your silence feel intentional—and earn curiosity instead of doubt?

反間計

33. Let the enemy's spies sow discord

Core Idea

This stratagem uses your opponent's own spy network to your advantage—by feeding them misinformation that creates internal distrust. Instead of simply blocking or avoiding espionage, you manipulate it to serve your goals. The name literally means "counter-espionage strategy," but it focuses on psychological warfare: turning the enemy's communication channels into a source of confusion and division.

The beauty of this strategy lies in its subtlety. You don't directly confront or attack your opponent; instead, you make them doubt their own people, leaders, or decisions. The internal chaos that follows weakens them from within, sometimes more effectively than any direct strike.

This approach is not only about military or political intelligence. In a modern context, it can apply to any situation where influence, reputation, or coordination matters—making it a powerful tool for competitive environments.

Historical Example

During the Warring States period, the state of Qin sought to weaken the alliance between the rival states of Zhao and Yan. Instead of fighting them head-on, Qin's advisors spread carefully crafted rumors—some reaching key officials in both states. The result? The alliance crumbled from mistrust, and the two states began suspecting each other of betrayal.

Qin then took advantage of the rift, conquering them one by one. Qin's ability to manipulate the internal dynamics of its enemies saved resources and time, while sowing just enough doubt to collapse the resistance from within.

Modern Marketing Scenario

You're a small but growing software startup. One of your larger competitors has recently acquired a trendy app, and the marketing world is buzzing with praise. But you've heard whispers that not everyone on their team is happy with the acquisition—it's created friction between their legacy team and the newly absorbed one.

Rather than attack them directly, you publish a case study on the challenges of post-acquisition culture clash, complete with anonymous quotes from "industry insiders." You run a podcast episode interviewing a founder who once sold their company and regretted how it was absorbed. You highlight the importance of internal harmony and creative freedom. All this content seems totally unrelated to your rival... but those inside the company know exactly what you're hinting at.

By letting internal doubts grow—subtly, indirectly—you make them more focused on managing their own turf wars than competing with you. You didn't invent the conflict. You just fanned the flames, and let their own people do the rest.

Practice Scenarios: Apply the Stratagem

Scenario 1: Influencer Irony

A competitor heavily promotes their partnership with a high-profile influencer. However, the influencer's personal posts complain about product reliability and communication breakdowns.

Your Challenge: How can you craft a subtle campaign that appeals to this influencer's followers without directly referencing the discord?

Scenario 2: Disgruntled Users Online

You discover threads on Reddit where long-time users of a competing app express frustration over a recent update.

Your Challenge: How can you surface those complaints in a respectful way—perhaps through your own community engagement or feature comparison—without looking like you're stirring the pot?

Scenario 3: Internal Team Drama Leaked

An ex-employee from a competing agency publicly shares that the leadership prioritizes flashy marketing over client results.

Your Challenge: How can your next marketing message position your brand as results-driven and client-focused, subtly contrasting your values with theirs?

苦肉計

34. Injure yourself to win the enemy's trust

Core Idea

This stratagem advises you to deliberately hurt yourself—or make a visible personal sacrifice—to gain the trust or sympathy of others. The goal is to create the illusion that you are innocent, loyal, or vulnerable so that your true intentions remain hidden. It's a bold tactic that uses self-inflicted losses as strategic bait.

The name literally means "the pain strategy" and comes from military history, where generals faked punishments or injuries to fool the enemy into lowering their guard. In modern terms, this means showing weakness or accepting short-term losses to secure a long-term gain.

It's not about deception for its own sake—it's about proving authenticity in ways others won't question. The best lies often wear the mask of honesty, and few things look more "honest" than personal suffering.

Historical Example

During the Three Kingdoms period, the strategist Huang Gai proposed to ally with the enemy Sun Quan by pretending to defect. To make it believable, he asked Zhou Yu to publicly beat him in front of the troops. The brutal punishment left Huang Gai bruised and bleeding—but it convinced the enemy Cao Cao that his defection was real.

As a result, Huang Gai was welcomed into Cao Cao's ranks. He later launched a surprise fire attack that burned Cao Cao's fleet, changing the tide of the Battle of Red Cliffs.

Without the painful setup, the deception would never have worked.

Modern Marketing Scenario

Sometimes the best way to gain your audience's trust is to admit your flaws. In a world saturated with polished marketing and inflated promises, showing vulnerability can make your brand appear more human and relatable. Imagine launching a new productivity app in a highly competitive market. Instead of pretending it's perfect, your landing page opens with:

"We used to waste hours tweaking to-do lists instead of getting things done. So we built this for ourselves first."

You also write a blog post titled, "3 Things Our App Still Sucks At," and follow up with how you're actively working to improve them. This type of radical honesty builds emotional credibility. When potential users see you're not trying to oversell, they're more likely to believe you when you say the app actually works. By exposing your own wounds, you lower their defenses—and gain their trust.

This isn't about fake humility. The self-inflicted 'injury' must be real enough to feel authentic. When done right, this stratagem can turn a disadvantage into a surprisingly strong brand advantage.

Practice Scenarios: Apply the Stratagem

Scenario 1: The Imperfect Founder Post

You're launching a niche writing tool, but your beta had bugs and lukewarm reviews. Instead of hiding it, you write a heartfelt post titled, "We Almost Gave Up." You talk about the setbacks, self-doubt, and how your team nearly quit—but also what pulled you through.

Your Challenge: How can you structure the story to feel vulnerable yet still lead users to root for your comeback?

Scenario 2: The Honest Sales Page

You're selling a course on how to go viral. You decide to begin the pitch with, "I wasted $5,000 on ads before learning this the hard way." You describe your failures in detail before introducing your system.

Your Challenge: How can you balance honesty about past failure without undermining your current credibility?

Scenario 3: Apologizing Before You're Accused

You just shipped a product with limited features due to time constraints. Instead of pretending it's fully ready, your email campaign reads: "This is not the full version. But it works. And we're improving it fast."

Your Challenge: How can you maintain excitement and trust while admitting your product's current limitations?

連環計

35. Chain stratagems together

Core Idea

This stratagem emphasizes combining multiple strategies in sequence to overwhelm, mislead, or outmaneuver an opponent. Instead of relying on a single tactic, you create a chain of interlocking moves—each one setting up the next.

It's a reminder that real mastery in strategy often comes from fluid, adaptive planning. One trick may be spotted, but a clever combination can be harder to predict and counter. This is especially useful in complex or prolonged situations where your opponent may recover if only one move is used.

Think of it like a magician's act: you distract the audience with one hand while preparing the real trick with the other. The first stratagem draws attention, the second weakens defense, and the third delivers the blow.

This method demands foresight, timing, and flexibility—and the ability to improvise as new developments unfold.

Historical Example

During the Three Kingdoms era in China, the strategist Zhuge Liang used a chain of deceptive moves to defeat his enemies. At one point, he deliberately abandoned supplies to lure his pursuers into a trap, used fake documents to spread misinformation, and finally ambushed the confused enemy at a narrow pass. Each step of his plan reinforced the next, and the full sequence only made sense in hindsight. If any one stratagem had been used alone, it might have failed—but together, they overwhelmed his enemies' ability to respond. This is the essence of a chain stratagem: calculated misdirection leading to decisive victory.

Modern Marketing Scenario

In today's marketing landscape, a single clever stunt rarely sustains attention for long. Consumers are flooded with distractions, and even the most brilliant idea can get buried in the scroll. That's where this stratagem comes in. Instead of relying on one trick, chain several strategic moves into a coordinated sequence.

Imagine launching a crowdfunding campaign for a niche productivity gadget. First, you leak an intriguing concept sketch on Reddit or Discord (Stratagem #7: Create something from nothing). Then, you collaborate with a micro-influencer who "discovers" your product and raves about it on YouTube (Stratagem #29: Flowers bloom on a borrowed tree). Next, you follow up with a limited beta program that invites only a few early adopters (Stratagem #28: Climb the roof and pull up the ladder). Finally, you open pre-orders with a "supply is limited" urgency play (Stratagem #4: Wait at ease for the weary enemy).

Each step builds curiosity, trust, exclusivity, and urgency— one stratagem after another—until the audience is too deep into your story to back out.

Practice Scenarios: Apply the Stratagem

Scenario 1: Stacked Micro-Campaigns

You're launching a new online course, but your audience is small and skeptical. You start by releasing a free worksheet that solves a niche pain point, then you host a short 3-day challenge, followed by a behind-the-scenes livestream, and finally open cart with a "founders-only" discount.

Your Challenge: Design a 4-step sequence using different stratagems that build anticipation and engagement in layers.

Scenario 2: Influencer + UGC Chain Reaction

Your indie board game needs traction. You seed a few early prototypes with content creators, each with a different spin—one focuses on the art, another on strategy, another on party fun. Then you repost player-generated content on your brand page and run a quiz that matches players to game roles.

Your Challenge: How would you script this content chain to create momentum without relying on paid ads?

Scenario 3: Launch Plan with Backup Triggers

You're about to launch a wearable tech product, but your team is worried one campaign might not be enough. You want a launch plan where if one thing fizzles, another kicks in. You've got influencer posts, a waitlist email blast, a "secret" landing page, and a local pop-up booth.

Your Challenge: Connect these actions with stratagems and explain how they interlock to reinforce the overall plan.

走為上計

36. If all else fails, retreat

Core Idea

This is the final and ultimate stratagem—when all other options are exhausted, the wisest move may be to walk away. Retreat isn't always cowardice; it can be a strategic decision to preserve strength, avoid destruction, and return to fight another day.

The idea is not to give up, but to recognize when a situation has become unsalvageable.

Staying in a losing battle can drain resources, morale, and future opportunities. A well-timed withdrawal is often the most courageous and intelligent move available.

This stratagem emphasizes adaptability, humility, and long-term thinking. It reminds us that survival and mobility are more valuable than pride or stubbornness.

Historical Example

During the late Tang Dynasty, military commander Li Keyong found himself surrounded by a coalition of enemies and betrayed by allies. Outnumbered and at a disadvantage, he decided to abandon his stronghold, retreating with a small, loyal force to safer territory.

His enemies believed he had been defeated. But after regrouping, Li returned with renewed strength and launched a successful counterattack that turned the tide. His choice to retreat wasn't a failure—it was the beginning of his rise to power.

Modern Marketing Scenario

Sometimes, the smartest move is to walk away—not out of fear, but out of strategic clarity.

You've launched a new app, poured months into development, built a campaign, and spent a chunk of your budget. But it's not working. The users aren't biting. The product-market fit isn't there. The temptation is to double down, tweak endlessly, and keep pushing because of all the effort and sunk cost.

But sometimes... it's better to retreat.

This stratagem doesn't mean giving up; it means redirecting your energy before you burn out or bankrupt yourself. Smart indie creators know when to cut losses and regroup. Maybe you rebrand. Maybe you pivot the product into a different niche. Or maybe you archive it entirely and take what you've learned into your next big idea.

Great marketers aren't just great at launching—they're also great at letting go.

Practice Scenarios: Apply the Stratagem

Scenario 1: The Sinking Side Hustle

You've spent six months developing a subscription-based productivity tool. The product works, but traction is low and customer feedback suggests there's just no strong need. You've already invested over $5,000.

Your Challenge: How do you evaluate whether it's smarter to pivot, pause, or walk away—despite the investment?

Scenario 2: The Partnership That Drains You

You partnered with an influencer to co-launch a product. At first, the exposure helped, but now the influencer is demanding more creative control and the brand direction no longer aligns with your values. You're constantly stressed and creatively blocked.

Your Challenge: How do you know when to step away from a collaboration, and how can you retreat gracefully without burning bridges?

Scenario 3: The Oversaturated Market

You've created a physical product that you later realized competes with dozens of near-identical items on Amazon. You're stuck in a race to the bottom on price, with slim margins and no brand differentiation.

Your Challenge: Do you keep optimizing and advertising, or is this the moment to withdraw and redirect your efforts into a less crowded battlefield?

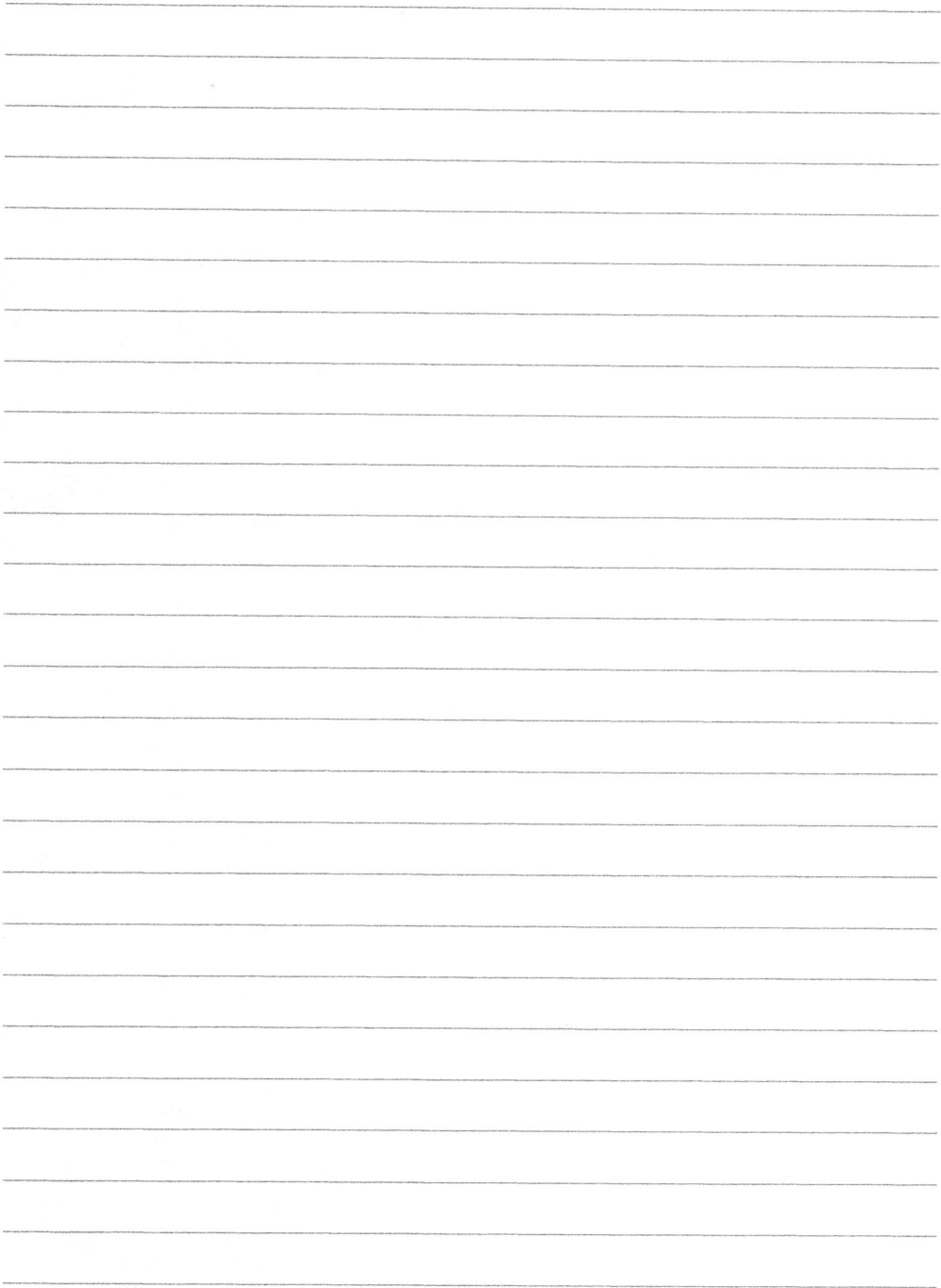

Afterword

Marketing is funny, isn't it?

You can read all the books, follow all the best practices, run all the experiments—and still, the market does whatever it wants.

I've seen this over and over again.

Even after years of working in startups, helping launch products with tight budgets and big ambitions, there's always that unpredictable factor.

Sometimes you're convinced something will work, and it falls flat. Other times, something small and unexpected takes off. And that's part of why I wanted to write this book.

Not because I have all the answers (far from it!), but because I love the idea of applying these old, clever, sometimes playful strategies to the messy, unpredictable world of launching and marketing a product.

I know, of course, that a book like this—about *The Thirty-Six Stratagems*—isn't exactly sitting in the hottest niche for English readers.

In fact, I've been aware of that from the start.

But I wrote it anyway.

Why?

Because I think these ideas are worth sharing, even if just a few readers find them and enjoy them.

So here's the irony:

After this book goes out into the world, I'll probably try some of the very strategies in this book to promote it.

Maybe they'll work.

Maybe they won't.

That's the beauty of this whole game: you never really know until you try.

But to me, that's what makes it meaningful.

Marketing isn't just about hacking attention or squeezing conversions—it's about sharing things you care about with people who might care too.

And even if only a handful of people discover this little book and feel inspired to think differently... well, that's enough for me.

So I hope you'll leave this book with a few new ideas, a few new ways to think, and a little spark of playfulness when you face your next product launch.

Good luck—and thank you for reading.

— Jimmy Lai

Colorado, USA

About the Author

I grew up in Taiwan and have published over a dozen books across Asia, mostly fiction. Even though writing has always been part of my life, I once went through a long stretch where I struggled to finish anything. It wasn't until after I moved to Colorado that I found my rhythm again—and this is the first series of books I've ever written in English.

Earlier in my career, I worked as a game developer. I left the industry after a mom called our office to complain that her child had used her credit card to buy a virtual item I designed. Since then, I've shifted my focus to education. These days, I work remotely, leading a team that builds learning platforms for the Taiwanese government. You could say I went from designing ways to level up game characters to designing tools that help real people level up.

I've always loved books about strategy—especially the kind that are rooted in real history, when one smart move changed everything. *The Thirty-Six Stratagems* is one of my favorites. Over the years, I've used it not just to think more clearly in everyday life, but also to build better twists and turns in the stories I write.

www.ingramcontent.com/pod-product-compliance
Lightning Source LLC
Chambersburg PA
CBHW022334280326
41934CB00006B/635